Are We
Almost Home?

A personal journey through the seasons of life on two continents, three US states, and 38 addresses.

In the cities and jungles. Among the impoverished and the wealthy. From birth to widowhood, all adventures with God by my side.

Shirley Alberta Roberts Combs

Other books by Shirley Combs:

THIS, THAT, and OTHER MIRACLES
WHO'S CLAPPING AT OUR GATE?
WOUNDED LAMBS NEED THE FOLD
THEY DESERVE A SECOND CHANCE
RICHARD'S RUN

Copyright @ 2022 by Shirley Alberta Comb
All right reserved. Churches and other non-commercial
interests may reproduce portions of this book without the
express written permission of the author provided that the
text does not exceed five percent of the entire book.

This book was printed in United States of America.

To order additional copies of this book, contact:
Shirley Combs
733 N.E. 18th Street
Moore, Oklahoma 73160

FWB
Editor, Layout and Cover Design:
FWB Publications, Columbus, Ohio

ISBN: 9798849815299 | Autobiography | Missionary

TABLE OF CONTENTS

1995, **Return to our home in Araras,** Serving three churches, and Children Home, Golden Shovel, Grand Dedication Church Planted in Jardim Candida, Church planted in Jardim Maraba' Family Highlights

1999, Owasso, OK With parents Mother, Heart Problems Father Changes Addresses To Wait or Not to Wait

Family Highlights Busy Training Time Short Trip to USA,

2004 Four more fruitful years Family Highlights – Babies and Weddings Mother Changes her Address Green Light! Photos, Family Photos

008, Culture Shock Re-entry Family Agenda Ministry Agenda Photos,   Family Photos

What's Behind the Bend? Winter Season Passion
My Winter Books of Miracles Photos,

To Kemper, Cindy, and Tânia, the three jewels of my life who are traveling on the same road to Home. Someone has said, It is not about the journey, but it is about the destination.

Okay, Our destination is HOME.

But on this journey,

"Be strong and of good courage, do not fear nor be afraid of them; for the Lord your God, He is the One who goes with you.

He will not leave you nor forsake you."

Deuteronomy 61:6

ACKNOWLEDGEMENTS

To all my readers who have believed in our wonderful Miracle Maker God and have shared their faith and their stories with others, I send my thanks.

Thanks to my son, Kemper, who proof-read these recorded life memories to help me remember important events, and to my go-to granddaughter, Julia, who cleaned up my 'X-rated' Amazon jungle photos. And to my patient grandson, Jacob, who helped me find my 'lost' photos. Once again, my sister-in-law, Judy Puckett, has helped me long-distance by phone and by my side.

A special thanks goes to my daughter, Tania. She is an avid reader and has encouraged me with great patience of many hours to complete these musings of my 80-year journey of adventures as seen from many addresses.

And to my beloved Savior Jesus Christ who has promised to be with me always. And He has.

FOREWORD

You're holding in your hand a legacy-a collection of stories drawn from the life and ministry of Shirley Roberts Combs. Each page was forged through decades of experience which allows you to sit down with such a pleasurable and profitable book--a book where you sit beside the author as if you walked with her.

This book is a book of thoughtful reflections, earned over multiple decades of obedience to her calling. Shirley shares in this beautiful memoir a discipleship journey. Blessings will await you in every chapter of her book.

Few women have ever walked across the landscape of her denomination and left such indelible footprints as Shirley Combs. Her broad range of experience and multifaceted ministry has had a profound impact on so many lives. Her book is a frank and honest story of a lady who truly loves the Lord. You will benefit by reading this account of how the Holy Spirit has led Shirley through many years of ministry as a true servant of Jesus Christ.

This book is by a lady who has had an extensive ministry among us, and her book is a testimonial that only she knew revealed in this wonderful autobiography. Her impact on many lives cannot be overstated. This book offers a reader the opportunity to trace God's hand at work and appreciate the heart of this outstanding lady. Already an author of four books you will find her life story one of a lady who had a multifaceted life. After reading this book you will fall in love not only with her but the Lord she serves.

Evidence of the powerful working of an omnipotent God permeates the pages. Those reading this compilation of stories surrounding the dynamic rescue of Brazil's street children undoubtedly will have their faith strengthened.

Shirley Combs is one of the most compassionate missionary servants I know. Her commitment and dedication to reaching the "social undesirables" of Brazil radiate from the pages of this book.

Dr. Alton E. Loveless

PREFACE

When I was younger, I wondered if I would make it to my Winter Season of Life. The young missionary men ministering to the Auca Indians, saw the glory of heaven before they ever reached their winter seasons. My young school friends, college mates, young relatives and missionary co-laborers didn't see their Winter Season.

My only brother, deacon and guitar playing teacher, didn't make it to his winter season in life. My two grandfathers didn't make it to their 50's. But their wives, my father, mother, sisters, and my husband did.

My publisher called one day suggesting I write my autobiography – to remember my adventures following God's plan. A gift to others. My excuses for not writing more books were that it was a lot of work and expensive, and a book about myself was embarrassing. After all, I AM in my winter season!

I had added a little of my life in my other four books, but they were mainly about the power of our miracle-maker God. I wrote about my husband, my children and grandchildren, and friends on two continents that intertwined with my own story. My valley experiences and my mountain top experiences all involved other people. But one common presence was my Lord Jesus.

Recently, a pastor in Texas, my nephew Randy Puckett, commented that people would rather read my story in one book than look for it in several. So that started me thinking.

God has chosen to give me strength and health enough to enjoy the adventures that continue to appear in my life.

Since widowhood I have suffered E.coli resulting from five years of cystocele, which caused an infection, which caused a high fever, which caused my daughter, Tania, to make an emergency stop to find a hospital on a return trip from a funeral in West Virginia.

There I was diagnosed with Sepsis and the hospital would not release me to continue our journey. Only after proof that we had an appointment with a doctor in Oklahoma on our arrival, would they reluctantly release me. Praise God I am here today!

The miracles I am still seeing must not be just for me. Should I continue to share? My desire is that my added years will be a gift to others.

Over and over again God's Word says to "remember," so I am a list maker, note taker, letter writer, journalist, and author. When I look back over my lists, notes, and books, I chuckle, rejoice, and get emotional over things I had forgotten. These days I need a method to help me remember why I left one room to enter another!

So, with God's help I can share with you the adventures of a common little nine-year-old girl from Oklahoma who surrendered to be used by a powerful God who did amazing things. All the recorded blessings are from God. I will choose not to give details on dark valley experiences in order to protect others involved and to protect the health of the Kingdom work.

To keep my facts straight, I will rely on diaries and notes and move on by years, seasons, and many addresses. Enjoy following my journey with an amazing Lord Jesus Christ.

Part One

MY SPRING SEASON

1942-1960

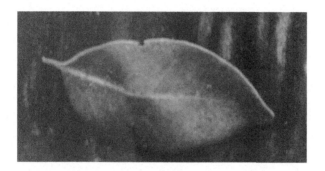

"O God, You have taught me from my youth;

And to this day

I declare your wondrous works."

Psalms 71:17

Chapter One

Springtime Season Begins

1942- Crowder, Oklahoma – a Winter Baby

At the end of the day, 15-year-old Marie was riding on the back of the wagon load of workers when the 19-year-old Thomas, the boss' son, jumped on the back of the wagon next to young Marie. Before the wagon stopped, Thomas threw a blanket over their heads and kissed her. Surprise! We children loved to hear that story.

My father, William Thomas Roberts, was the youngest son of a preacher, Albert Roberts and wife Norah. His father hired field workers at harvest time. My mother, Lucy Marie Laughlin, was the oldest daughter of a widow lady, Winnie Myrtle Laughlin, and was working to help her family.

Father later sent Mother a letter telling her that he really wanted to marry her. She and her mother consented, and he sealed his intentions by giving her a ruby ring.

Young Marie had worked at other jobs to help support her four siblings orphaned of a father. At 12 she worked for a doctor and was declared a good worker. But the doctor's daughter didn't want her, the hired help, to sit with the family at meal time. So, 12-year-old Marie sat alone to eat. It hurts me to imagine the scene.

But another thing happened when she was 12, praise God! She went to a revival service in a brush harbor near the Perry Free Will Baptist church meeting in the school house, near Stigler, Oklahoma. The preacher she called Papa Yandell. I remember that he was a guest in our home many times. She was touched by a Lord that showed her worth that helped her be a soul winner and a wonderful Christian mother to all of us.

Young Thomas had not actually surrendered to Christ until he was 19, after meeting my mother. He knew God was calling him to preach so at conversion he surrendered to salvation and to ministry.

He and mother married and started their family. Since at that time churches did not pay full-time salaries, he was bi-vocational while preaching at several churches. Microphones were not used in churches at that time and preacher Tom Roberts did not need one! He had a strong singing bass voice and my mother an outstanding alto voice. They would pass a love for music to their children.

Welcome, Baby Number Five

By the time I was born, their family of four children had moved to Crowder, Oklahoma. Mother was expecting me, her fifth child at about 28 years old. My father was working for the government by building roads during World War II. They had three daughters, Loretta Murl Dean, Phillis Alene, Velma Dolores, and one boy, Wayne Thomas. At that time, you could not know the gender of the unborn child, so they had chosen to name this child after the paternal grandfather, Preacher Albert.

My Spring Season of life was about to begin. Guess what? It was winter time! It was the night of the 14th of January, 1942. There was so much snow and ice on the ground that they could not get to the hospital in Stigler and the doctor could not get to their house in Crowder. Even though mother had birthed four children already, everyone saw that she was struggling in her increasing birth pains. They called a neighbor lady to help and shewed all the men and children out of the room.

On my first winter season, I was born at 10 pounds. Not easy for the young mother who really needed a doctor present, as my aunts told me. But my mother claimed the scripture that once each child was in her arms, she forgot about the pain. And since I was a girl, they changed the name from Albert to Alberta! (Since the Elberta peaches and Alberta sounded familiar, my nickname became "Peaches".) Shirley Alberta Roberts was welcomed by a nervous father and four curious siblings. My three older sisters told me later that they had been told that babies came from the little black bag the doctors carried. There was no doctor nor black bag that winter night, so they were surprised to hear a baby cry from the next room.

I don't know how long we lived in Crowder. I remember falling as a preschooler from a porch swing nailed to the edge of the porch. I fell to the grass at the edge of the porch and cut my lip on a small Prince Albert metal can. I guess I remember it from the stories they told me while pointing to the scar on my lip. The house was blown away by a tornado so I never saw it again.

Stigler, Oklahoma –, First and Second Grades, 1947

"House Near the Tracks"

I remember three houses where we lived in Stigler, Oklahoma. The first I remember was referred to as the "one near the tracks." If my memory serves me correctly, it was small and the siding was asbestos shingles. I have learned they were more resilient to weathering, not like the softer shingles. They were made of asbestos cement board. We had an outhouse behind the house and we heated water on the stove for different things. We fetched water from the pond for bathing and other cleaning.

Our three older sisters were adolescents and teens. By that time there was the sixth addition to the family. Our baby sister, Carolyn. Our maternal grandmother ran a hotel when mother was about to give birth, so she went to stay with her mother at the hotel until Wanda Carolyn was born on July 14th. One and a half years to the day younger than I. So, my brother, Wayne, was about six, and Carolyn was three and I was four. We played with other neighborhood children who were poor, too, and we didn't know it. So, life was good.

The house was full of family and we were as contented as anyone else. One memory stands out because our paternal grandmother Roberts and great-grandmother Wyatt visited us one day. Great grandmother was blind so Carolyn and I were assigned to take her hands and guide her to the outhouse out back. Today, I wonder if she had cataracts and there were no treatments for those at that time or no funds for such.

Another memory of great grandmother Wyatt was at her funeral. My sister and I were sitting on a church pew and crying. Everyone else was, so we did, too. Someone on the pew behind us quietly passed a stick of gum to each of us. We just looked at the flat piece wrapped in paper since we had never had anything like that. We had seen bubble gum, which couldn't be chewed in church, but this was different. Well, the lady's idea worked. We put the gum quietly in our mouths and stopped crying immediately!

Our house was near the railroad track and we made it a point to watch the afternoon train pass and wave at the engineer. We would gather little chunks of coal that fell from the trains, and for some reason our mother was thankful for them. We had never even seen an airplane before and there were as many horses and buggies as there were cars. So, that tremendous, noisy monster machine was a fascinating sight for our young eyes. We were about three, four, and six years old.

One day as we waved, the engineer threw things from his window and waved as the objects fluttered to the ground. We looked at each other and then ran toward the objects. Comic books. Real, colorful comic books!! We had never held such treasurers in our own hands. We were too young to read, but how proudly we could show others. I wonder now how long the dear engineer planned on seeing three little blue eyed, barefoot children receive his presents. Maybe his own books or maybe his children's. A gift in the Spring season of my life that I still remember in my winter season.

One not-so- good memory, but a great lesson learned, was about the only time I remember my father spanking us. Remember, we were three, four, and six. One day we went into a wooded area where we always played with other children. There was a persimmon tree. Maybe we didn't let the tiny fruits get ripe, but they were terrible. They put our teeth on edge, but we were challenged to eat them green. (When I had a persimmon tree at my own home in Brazil, I could hardly believe that beautiful red, juicy, round, sweet fruit with a texture like a grape but the size of a large apple had the same name. It was delicious. Wonderful!)

When we returned from playing, Mother and Father were waiting for us. Uh oh. Too serious. They called the three of us and said they had a sad report about our group in the woods that day. They were told that some child was "mooning" us. True, and we certainly didn't tell them we thought that was naughty, but funny. Oh, no, that wouldn't help.

I soon learned that my four-year-old body was important to my parents and to God and that spanking was to help us remember to not be "naughty". But in another city at the home of some playmates, at a rare moment when I was alone, a family friend hugged me from the back and placed his hands inside my clothes and touched me inappropriately. He wasn't my mommy or my doctor so I twisted free! Later as an adult, I realized I had forgiven him as I looked at his folded hands in his casket.

"Bloody Bucket"

The next house must have been during hard times. The nation was still recovering from WW II, but like I said, we children didn't feel it. Somehow, we had food, clothes, family and were not school age so we had time to play with cousins. And our next house was full of cousins.

That house was called the "Bloody Bucket". It was a Quonset hut that had been bought from military surplus for public use. It was a lightweight prefabricated structure of corrugated galvanized steel. It had once been bought for a bar and painted red. Thus, the nickname "Bloody Bucket".

The ex-bar now was our Aunt Wanda's home and she invited our family, my mother's sisters Reba and their families to live together with her family. I remember curtains were hung to divide off the sections for the families. Our father was now a builder and preached at a different church each Sunday. At the same time, we believe he was building us a home in the country outside of Stigler.

Diamond-W Home

Our land out in the country was up a slight slope next to the gravel road passing through the section. The trees and brush had to be cleared to build our house that looked like a beautiful mansion in my eyes. Our father had placed shutters on the front windows with a diamond-W design on them. That is how we named it our 'Diamond-W" home. Our oldest sister, Loretta Murl-Dean, had married so there were five children and my parents to occupy our new home.

Our father had built an impressive indoor bathroom. He wired for electricity, and indoor plumbing for the kitchen. BUT we were in the country without electricity and water. So, we dug a well and learned to draw it daily. We learned to light and clean kerosene lamps daily. We had a big, black pot belly stove to keep us warm in cold weather. We had our first fancy ice-box. (Not an electric refrigerator.) The ice man passed by on certain days and we put a sign in the window to order the size of ice block we wanted that day. We kept the long ice tongs ready for when we needed it.

There were three bedrooms. The girl's bedroom was large enough for us four girls with two full size beds and dresser. Dolores and Carolyn on one bed and Alene and I on the other. Through the years our father could make us beautiful furniture, too, and mother amazing quilts for each bed.

That place was full of adventure and stubs where we stubbed our bear toes! Among the trees in the back of the house was an Indian graveyard. There were markers and one small area was separated by a metal lattice fence. The graves looked sunken. We imagined it was a family plot and wondered where their ancestors were. All around us we found stone arrow heads. Just imagine if we had saved them to have now.

From there we have a lot of inside jokes and stories of our childhood and it is special in their simplicity, but of a special time when children were children. There were grape vines and yes, my brother would swing on them. He said some of the boys said they were good to smoke. Never knew if he tried some. We tease our little sister about her fantasizing with trees as friends. One day she was hugging and kissing them when she was attacked by ants!

Wayne had already started to school and had a friend at the nearest house through the trees. One day they were looking at his friend's new BB gun and I could see them through the clearing. It was a new toy that we had heard about, but only seen in magazines. Bobby Dean was shooting at soap bubbles with his new toy. Well, I was far away, but somehow when he shot the little spherical bullet at a soap bubble it reached all the way to me and   lodged in my right eye. It soon came out of my eye, but the story of the amazing power to travel so far of that new little "toy" spread through conversations of adults and children. Soon the BB gun became popular on children's Christmas lists. That goes to show you that people are right when they say "be careful that BB gun can shoot your eye out!"

Speaking of toys, even though plastic had already been invented, the common families didn't have it yet. During WWII it was used for parachutes, body armor, helmet liners, and ropes. After living through the Great Depression and the war, Americans started buying items of plastic. However, it took a while for it to reach the Roberts family. Just wood, metal, glass and ceramics.

But the folks did dig out a shallow trench far in the back yard to place the used cans and broken ceramics and glass. We played store keeper and retrieved the cans and placed our "merchandise" on old wooden crates. We learned to bargain with our fake money.

The only time we went to town was on Saturdays when the folks went to the market in Stigler. They give us children a quarter to go to the Saturday matinées with a bag of popcorn and a coke. A real treat. It had two theaters – The Place and The Time. Both were on the same block and same side of the street.

We had a cow and calf named Judy and Jane, named after characters from a radio program Mother liked. Our one pig a year always brought friends over to butcher and prepare for us and for friends. It was salted down and put in the cellar.

I became of school age at this house. There was no kindergarten at that time, so my father took me to first day of school at Stigler Boon Grade School. I still remember the beautiful box of eight Crayola's on my first day and found out that I loved school! The next year my little sister started first grade and I the second. Our brother and sisters rode the school bus with us. The school bus picked us up in front of our country house and years later a young man, George Aery, who rode with us on that bus as children met up with my younger sister in California and MARRIED her!

That was the year a little boy in my class offered to give me one of his dog's puppies if my father would go pick it up at his house. We did and the dog, Skeeter, moved with us to several cities as I was growing up. It was the first time I had ever been teased about a boy. Wish I could remember his name!

Each Sunday we went with our parents to churches where our Father preached. He had four churches so each Sunday we attended one. I remember the folks were so nice to our large family. I loved the "card classes" as ours were called and we received small cards with a Bible picture on the front and the story on back. I thought it would be so wonderful to grow up and teach from little cards like those. And one day I did.

One church was in a school house with a black pot belly stove and was located in the country. A family with children our ages invited us to eat with them since it was a long drive back home. It was so special to play all afternoon while the adults visited.

My little sister and I would sing duets. You can't lose with little children singing, I know. But my sister could harmonize with her alto part. Now that made it different! We said that she was the last to sit on mother's lap and learned from her beautiful, strong alto voice.

Our father stood us up on the wooden chairs they used back then, right up front so we could be seen as we sang. We were five and six years old. One Sunday at the Crossroads Free Will Baptist Church in Stigler, we were already up front on the chairs and we were to begin with the song, "He Set Me Free"

Carolyn turned to me and whispered in my ear. I shook my head no and she insisted on whispering again. Mother said, "Girls straighten up now and sing. The people are waiting."

I looked at Carolyn and back to my mother, "But mother, she wants to sing 'I didn't Know God Made Honkytonk Angels'"

Carolyn looked up and said in her little voice, "But it has God and angels in it. Why can't we sing it?"

The whole church seemed to smother giggles and turn in their chairs. Well, we ended up singing "He Set Me Free" and it has become one of the family's favorite stories.

After Carolyn married and had a family, she and her husband and children formed a singing group and made recordings that reached many people!

Times were difficult for people those years and some could not pay our Father much. But that didn't make a difference to him and my mother. They served anyway. They loved on them as family – which they were. Many times, when we left the churches, they would give us eggs and chickens. Produce from their gardens. A freshly baked loaf of bread.

Sometimes our Father would invite the whole congregation to the house for a fried chicken dinner. Mother would just shake her head and smile. She was a great hostess and usually already had part of the meal prepared before we went to church. Church ladies would go right to the kitchen and help cook and it was a great time for everyone.

We children never felt uneasy about finances. When he wasn't looking, we saw our father wire the soles onto his work shoes a few times. But they shared their stories with us when God came through to provide and bless their faithfulness. We always felt secure that God knew our family and would provide.

The whole family would go to brush harbor meetings with lots of preaching, singing, and hallelujahs. Everyone sat on backless benches, so as her children went to sleep during the long, but lively services, I remember Mother spread a pallet on the sawdust covered ground so we could sleep. She had six children at that time, but she always seemed proud of us.

Decoration Day each year meant another meeting with friends. During the school vacation, I would go to my Grandmother Winnie Myrtle Wilson's house and she taught me how to make beautiful crepe paper flowers. She was a widow for the third time and she sold many of her flowers.

After the folks decorated the graves of relatives and then stood around talking about the lives of each one, there was a chapel at the cemetery and many people met there to sing and give testimonies.

One of our favorite preachers was Brother Leonard Crowder. We loved his family, too. He must have been a special friend because he performed the wedding of my sister Dean with Herbert Hale. One of our favorite stories from his sermons was "boots or no boots." He said some men promised new boots if he could preach a sermon without saying so loudly the words 'Amen'. Well, he said he tried it but got so blessed that he couldn't hold it in. So, all of a sudden during the sermon he shouted, "Amen, boots or no boots."

After the singing time, table cloths were spread on the ground or boards were set on saw horses. The adults and children would unload covered dishes from their cars or horse and buggies and dinner would be served after prayer.

One Decoration Day that I especially remember I ended up in the hospital. I was carrying food to a shaded place under a tree where other children were seated. There were no paper plates and cups at that time, so I was balancing my China plate of food and tea in a jelly glass with my eyes on the group waiting under the tree.

I tripped on some small roots jutting out of the ground. I don't know what my head hit, but it cut a gash in my forehead and blood started streaming quickly. The children screamed for help. My father carried me to the backseat of our car where my Grandmother Wilson was waiting for me. I remember I had my head in her lap and her beautiful white laced hanky was covered in red. Mother drove us to a doctor in town where I got some stitches. I can touch my tiny scar as I write this and memories come back to mind. We had many childhood memories in Stigler.

Then one day it happened.

We had a crank telephone hanging on the wall of our new Diamond-W home. A party line with several other families. It was up to each one to decide if they were going to "listen in" on other people's calls. Our number was two longs and one short. That meant long crank turns and short crank turns.

One week we had a young preacher as a guest in our home for a few days. He had come to Oklahoma from North Carolina and we children loved his accent. He would trot us on his knees and makes us laugh. His name was Wade Jernigan and he and Tommy Roberts became friends. After he had returned to Tulsa for a few days, he called us on our phone. Mother was listening to the one-sided conversation, maybe also some people on the party line, and understood that it was an invitation of some kind to move to somewhere.

She said, "Oh, dear. We finally just moved into our house and have these church families. Oh, dear."

But after the conversation continued, she ended up saying, "Tell him yes, we will do it if that is God's will."

Brother Wade had gone back to his church and recommended our father and mother to shepherd the church.

The Roberts family moved again and God had new adventures for us.

Berryhill, Oklahoma – Third and Fourth Grades, 1950

After receiving the phone call from Preacher Wade Jernigan, I am sure there was much packing and selling things, but I just remember arriving in Berryhill, Oklahoma, and seeing the New Home Free Will Baptist Church.

Since I didn't know of any church in our area that paid their pastor full-time, the idea of living in a parsonage right next to the church was luxury to me. We were a family of six children, and a grandchild. My oldest sister's husband was in the Navy so she and the baby lived with us for a while. They now have a much larger, modern parsonage, but Mother did miracles and made it a little house with a big heart.

It is west of Tulsa, Oklahoma, but is an unincorporated community and is approximately four-square miles in area. I remember seeing a school right in front of the church, go Chiefs! A service station/convenient store, and it looked small. But it became a focal point in my life story.

As usual for them, my parents were active in the denominational efforts in the area. They volunteered to help in the First Mission Camp Grounds for many years. That way I was able to attend camps before I was camp age. Sis. Cleo Purcell taught a class on Stewardship which was full of missionary challenge. Each year as I grew, I heard pastors and evangelists that would stir my little soul.

Recently I saw a plaque at the Wood Creation store that read, "A child is not a vessel to be filled, but a lamp to be lit." Well, I think that my parents did fill my vessel. They filled me with a love of God, His Holy Word, God's creation around us, and a love for people. Then at the age of nine years old, on a Wednesday night at New Home church, with young L.A. Yandell preaching, the Holy Spirit lit my lamp and I have that fire still burning in me until now during my Winter season.

Carolyn, my younger sister went with me to the altar. My third-grade teacher, Sis Elsie Hargis, was there, kneeling by me at the altar saying. "Give it all, Shirley. Ask Him to forgive you and save you, and that you will live for Him with your whole heart." I did! My brother Wayne, my sister Carolyn, and I were baptized in a little creek somewhere in the community. I remember that the next day everything was much brighter. (Like the day after I recently had cataract surgery.) I asked my playmates if they had heard my good news. They had.

Sister Elsie Hargis put the 100th Psalm on her classroom blackboard for her third-grade class. We repeated it daily for a year and it is still written on my memory until today. I remember that I wanted to be a teacher one day just like her. One day it happened.

She and my mother became good friends, worked in the church, and sang together in a quartet. After my husband and I went to Brazil she sent offerings to our account until her death. My father preached, "Either you Send, or you Go!" I always felt that she and others who sent us participated in every soul saved and baptized, every abandoned child that was rescued, every seed of hope that we planted. Public teachers have great influence.

Go-Tell Auxiliary for girls, Youth League meetings, and all the regular church services and activities helped us grow spiritually. Another child from my class and that church became a pastor, Odell Nunley. Another young person who grew up in that same church is now a missionary with his family, Jacob Myers. His wife is a M.K. (missionary kid), of the Darrell Nichols family. Two of my best heart friends from my church and school were Barbara Woolsey and Marjorie Wooldridge. Because we were continents and 5,000 miles apart, we have not seen each in other in 70 years. Bless be the tie that binds! The young Charles and Margarete Hinsley couple became "adopted" by my folks and were active in the church. They named one of their girls after my mother. There were so many more. Oh, to be a part of God's family!

One Christmas I participated in the grade school Christmas play as the angel declaring the good news of Christ's birth. I had to memorize many scriptures and it was an emotional experience. I continued to participate in church drama in my spiritual growth, and on the mission field I wrote and directed church drama for 44 years! Public schools can reinforce the faith growth of children and of families and help create lasting memories. The school needs that privilege.

Other positive family memories from our childhood there are still with me. Just small, sweet memories. We placed a quilt at night on the grass in the front lawn of the parsonage. Lying on our backs we gazed up at the stars in wonder.

We walked up the road to the house of a friend and saw our very first television. Roy Rogers and Dale sang "Happy Trails" as they solved problems and the Lone Ranger and Tonto, rode off with a "Hi-O Silver," as thankful people waved. All in black and white on a small screen as we sat on the floor.

A Singing School teacher came to the church and taught shaped notes, do-re-mi, and counting the beats. My brother got a horse, but it was kept somewhere else. I learned a few basic chords on the piano. The folks bought a used bike and painted it and presented it for all of us to share. Our older sisters started dating boys. A deacon sneaked out of church and placed gifts under the Christmas tree for us. Mine and Carolyn's was a doll and a carriage.

Relatives from hours away came with our cousins and we had watermelon, homemade ice cream, and played outside until dark. Ah, sweet memories of childhood!

Sapulpa – Fifth Grade and Sixth grade, 1st semester, 1952

Our house in Sapulpa was on a street in a nice neighborhood. It was a new experience for me since I didn't remember being surrounded by other houses and families before then. I liked it. It was a small house, too, and our brother had his bed in a little porch that was closed in for him. The whole street was lined on both sides with big trees. Our older sister, Alene, was already married and our sister Dolores was in Sapulpa High School. I remember that she worked as a car-hop at an A&W Root Beer place. We loved to hear the stories about her good tips.

Jefferson Grade School was just down the street on which we lived. Carolyn and I could walk to school. My dog, Skeeter, followed us until we were close to the school, returned and then waited for us to return home. Neighborhoods were safe and children could go on long walks around the neighborhood by themselves.

One special memory was a meeting of the entire school in the auditorium of Jefferson Grade School. After we were seated, we noticed a tiny black and white television on a table sitting on the stage at the end of the auditorium. We had never had one.

There was no microphone when the principle spoke, but at that time students were quiet and respectful so we strained to hear. If we didn't observe rules, we had consequences at school and then from our parents when we arrived home. We were taught to respect authority. We felt safe and life was good.

The special occasion was for all of us to observe the inauguration of our new president. Five-star General Dwight David Eisenhower. Our 34th president. He served from 1953 to 1961. He was nicknamed "Ike". We felt the excitement of the moment. We knew it was a special day. We were North Americans, living in our good country and we were proud of it, and, we had never seen an inauguration! That is a good basis on which children can grow. Safe. Positive. Appreciative.

I was in a class of 45 children. Our teacher read a chapter to us each day after our work was done. The "Box Car Children" book kept our attention and we never wanted her to stop reading. We admired the courage and ingenuity of the orphan children and it left its mark on me and I was reminded of it years later.

Another memory is an assignment the teacher gave us to choose a country and make a report about it. No google help at that time, but we had amazing reference books and encyclopedias. I chose the country of Brazil and designed a tropical cover for it. About 10 years later my mother showed it to me two days before my wedding. She had saved it all those years because she said she "knew" God was already calling me to be a missionary. And it might be Brazil. Well, she was right. Less than two years later my husband and I landed in Brazil as career missionaries.

Each child had his or her turn to be a crossing guard and to wear the yellow safety sash. It was a proud day when it was my turn to help folks cross the street near the school. Also, I was proud when after watching the boys play marbles during recess, one of them gave me one that was called "steely". The other marbles were made of colorful glass. Then another day he gave me one more "steely".

When my brother saw them, he teased, "Shirley has a boyfriend. Shirley has a boyfriend, now." I denied it and didn't understand. He said that it was a very important marble and the boy wouldn't have given it too just anybody. Something about a "taw" and leader marble. Wow, I certainly didn't understand boys!

Our folks had church family friends, the McVales, who lived in the neighborhood within walking distance. Guess what? They had a television and invited us to watch "I Love Lucy" and the new "Howdy Doody Show". We fell in love with the puppet Howdy Doody, the clown Clinker Bell, and Buffalo Bob who taught us basic life lessons in the western theme. It was the first televised children's show to air in our country. And long lasting, from 1947 to 1960. It had children in the audience singing "It's Howdy Doody Time". And who could forget the talking cereal, "Snap, Crackle, Pop" Rice Krispies? I know now how special and patient that couple was to open their home to three young preacher kids.

Tulsa – Sixth Grade, 2nd semester, and Seventh, 1st Sem.1954

One of the main streets in Tulsa, Oklahoma, was Sheridan Avenue and that was our next address. My sister Dolores wanted to finish her senior year in Sapulpa, so she stayed with family friends, the McVales, for her last semester.

Our house was covered with beautiful large rocks, large trees, and it had more room than the last one. It had an apartment in the back of the property and my sister Alene and her family lived there.

Since I really enjoyed school, I adapted quickly to the Junior High there. I remember receiving recognition for penmanship and perfect attendance. There were a couple of family memories that were a little sad, though.

One was that my sister Carolyn had to miss a lot of school. She had throat trouble and it was diagnosed polio and they treated her for that. But finally, another doctor diagnosed Rheumatic Fever. They assigned her a home-bound teacher. Her teacher and classmates did something that I have copied since. They sent her cards and simple presents and marked a day of the week on each one. She looked forward each day to opening one after she did her homework. It helped pass the time until she was able to go back to school.

The second sad memory is of that day I returned from school and called to Skeeter, my dog. The folks said he had died that morning with rheumatism in his hips. He was my first dog and companion. It hurt too much and I wondered if I could ever have a pet dog again! Years later in Brazil, I did.

Another novelty at that house was since our Father was a preacher, complete strangers would arrive at the door wanting to get married. They would be interviewed, asked for the documents, and went through the ceremony and said "I do." It was the first time I saw anyone pay my father for performing a wedding.

There was another wedding while we were in that house. My sister Dolores finished high school and came to our house in Tulsa for about a week. We remember the hustle and bustle of those days before the beautiful bride and her groom, Loy Shivers, were married in the New Home Free Will Baptist Church.

Our Father and family were asked to help with the new mission church that would soon be the Airport Free Will Baptist Church, in Tulsa. It is now a beautiful church on North Mingo. Another church I saw in its infancy and it is close to my heart.

Claremore – Ninth grade, 1957

Ahh, Claremore. There are so many memories from here as I entered my first teenage years. Some **first**-time things. By that time, two of my sisters married military men who then studied in colleges. One sister and her family lived in Claremore.

Our Father had accepted the challenge to revitalize the Free Will Baptist Church there situated in a nice neighborhood. I remember living in an upstairs apartment for **the first** time while he built a parsonage next to the church. I shaved my legs for the **first** time in that apartment, too, and cut a gash in my leg! Small teenage memories.

Parsonage life.

The parsonage was a three-bedroom home that opened its doors to many people. I remember that Papa Yandell was a welcomed guest and was going blind. So, while sitting on the back steps with him, I was honored to read for the **first** time for him the scriptures he was going to use in his next sermon.

Anytime denominational representatives were close by in meetings, and when home and foreign missionaries were in the area, they seemed to end up in our parsonage and enjoying my dedicated mother's wonderful meals. I listened through the open doors at night to hear for the **first** time of God's power in planting churches around the world.

A special meal was shared at the parsonage with a couple who had sung at the same convention as my parents. They were so interesting and handsome. It was my **first** chance to share a meal with black Christians.

Oh, yes, I got my **first** kiss by a boy who pulled me behind a door during a church meeting. He was a tall preacher's kid and I had barely even talked to him! He lived in another city so we hardly saw each other after that.

Another friend drove his convertible all the way from Norman, Oklahoma, to Claremore to visit. Surprise! We took him to visit the largest Totem Pole in the state, the Will Rogers influence in the city, and the largest gun museum at that time. I met him when I visited my sister in Norman and he had gotten me started saving lead pennies. I eventually had a gallon full. I was too young to date and he didn't have the same faith as I, but I still got a lot of teasing. No, we never shared a kiss, but I did have my **first** convertible ride.

Ministry Assignment

I was given my **first** Sunday School teaching assignment. The small children's "card class!" Our family left out early Sunday mornings to go to the Radio Station in Pryor, Ok. We were a singing family and had enough members to sing harmony to Gospel evangelistic songs and hymns. But this was the **first** time on radio! Good music helped spiritual growth. It was the **first** time we had an electrical guitar in our church band.

Some special people in church were from a full blood Cherokee family. George Locust, wife Bertha, and two daughters. The father taught the youth and taught me to drive a standard shift car for the **first** time. His wife invited Carolyn and me to their house for the evening meal, but they ate early at 4:00 pm! Their two daughters were our best Christian friends. I remember an example Bro. George used several times to the youth.

"If you have a young calf and lift it up each day without fail, as the calf grows, your strength will grow. That is the way with the Christian walk. Each day you read the Word without fail and you will gain spiritual strength." True advice.

When I took my driver's test, I was prepared. But I was asked for my birth certificate for the **first** time. However, I was never registered! But Mother had gone prepared and opened the family Bible to the page that registered information of my birth. The policeman looked at the page and then at me.

"I can accept this if you will answer one question. Where can we find the Ten Commandments in this Bible?" he asked.

Maybe since we had just had a week of camp studying the Ten Commandments, I answered quickly, "Exodus, chapter 20".

The policeman smiled, my mother relaxed, and I could breathe again. Yes! My driver's test was on its way.

Schools.

My brother was a junior in Claremore High School. I was in the freshmen class and in the first group to occupy the new Will Rogers Junior High Building in 1957. Carolyn was in Grade School. I sang in the school choir, I worked in Principle Denny's office, was a member of the Pebble Pups Club because I wasn't old enough to be a member of the Rock Hounds, and loved every class I had. One day I was selling items door to door to raise money for a school project. I had the most sales, but a little dog took a big bite out of my calf! I didn't love that!

Our family heritage was Irish/Dutch from Europe. I had gone to school with native Indians and black students, but I had not had the chance to be in class and really get to know them. For the **first** time I made friends with a mixture that prepared me for what God had planned for the future. I cherish their friendships. Thanks, Claremore. Go Zebras!

One special instructor was my history teacher. He encouraged me to enter a state wide essay contest about Oklahoma. I chose the subject of the State Seal as seen on our beautiful flag and entered it. It took so long to receive an answer that I hardly remembered it. One day my teacher showed me a letter to the school announcing that I had won **first** place in the state. He shared that he thought I had a gift in writing and should develop it. And here I am in my Winter Season writing again.

Young Employment.

A single-parent father was a neighbor and was looking for help. He needed to leave for work before his two small daughters caught the school bus. He asked our folks if Carolyn and I could stay with the girls until the bus arrived. They consented.

Wow! Our **first** paid job. One of the girls was deaf-mute and we placed a piece of her hearing device in a little halter around her neck and under her clothing. It was satisfying to help the children before we went to our schools. Little Glenda and Sandra were sweet darlings. It caused us to be thankful for our own health.

Some neighbors asked the folks if I could work at their Title and Abstract Office in downtown Claremore. They had consulted the school and they recommended me based on my scholastic record of straight A's for the last six years. (Blush). My parents agreed.

My **first** official office job. We sat side by side on tall stools at tall tables with huge, thick books. We registered the exact location of a certain property that could later be researched by a real estate company, by builders, or by lawyers writing up wills or divorce documents, or buyers who wanted to be sure there are no defects in the registration of the property to be purchased.

Whew! It was really a responsibility. And I was only 15. But I liked the challenge. We placed small checks in tiny boxes on pages of huge books by hand of exact locations of properties that would be accepted as proof of truth. Mistakes would be serious. Mental and physical pressure was with us daily.

We were certainly ready for our afternoon breaks! For the **first** time I purchased with my own money glass coke bottles from a machine and little bags of peanuts to pour into the bottles. Well, everyone was doing it and today I like to put peanuts in my orange juice.

Great memories, but there was a new place to go.

The church was growing, the parsonage would help the church to provide better for the next pastor, and there were trained church members to help carry on the work.

Owasso, Oklahoma – 1958

Owasso was a city of a population of about 450 when our Father started placing curbs and gutters on the city streets. He also built neighborhoods of new homes that attracted new families. The population today at this writing is an estimated 38,450.

There was no Free Will Baptist Church there and our family had a desire to be a part of planting one there. We moved from Claremore into one of the new homes our Father built in Owasso and started a new chapter of our lives.

Schools

All three of us were in Owasso School. It was a campus right downtown with one building for first to twelfth grades and an auditorium for sports, graduations, and other activities. A nice football field and bleachers were at the other end of town. We were soon active in a small-town school. Go Rams!

I was chosen as a cheerleader and formed great friendships. It was a small school so we cheered at football games, baseball games, and basketball games. The same athletes participated in the other sports. They were also the same ones who were officers of Future Farmers of America and Future Homemakers of America. Advantages of a small school.

At school we pledged allegiance to our flag, sang the National Anthem, and prayed. Patriotism was practiced, work ethics were taught, pride in our city growth and conservation was observed, and church attendance was a normal thing in our town.

The students voted me as their Student Body president and the vice president was a nice Christian boy. We tried to be good testimonies and improve student life. It was a good thing that physical beauty wasn't a priority in contests because I was elected Owasso Princess to participate in a parade in Tulsa and was runner up for Football Queen. (It may have helped that I had dated some of the players!) Go Rams!

Our choir took a field trip to Tulsa to hear the philharmonic orchestra. Our conductor asked me to send in an essay on the performance for a state-wide contest. I sent it in. The school received a notice that their student, Shirley Roberts, had won first place and was asked to go to the next performance to receive a recognition. My parents went with me on stage and I was so proud and thankful for them because they were always supportive of all of their children in our school activities.

For three years I was in the school plays and created an interest in visual productions. It was very useful in my future calling as a missionary.

Church: A deacon and family from Keota, near Stigler, moved into town and had a Free Will Baptist background, Homer and Beulah Brown and their two high school aged son, Jim Carlos and Tilton. Another FWB family moved to town, the Foy Testermans with three children in their teens, Jim, Nell, and Jesse. With a small group praying about a local church, interest started growing.

After services held in temporary places (ex., abandoned theater, old fire station, etc.) a group was forming. A young pastor was called to lead, Don Payne, and stayed a short time. After he left, the folks voted for our father to continue the work. The group was organized as the Free Will Baptist church in Owasso.

My father led the men in constructing the church building on North Atlanta located downtown. Mother organized an active women's group, Women's Auxiliary, whose focus was on missions, Christian education, benevolent community outreach, and needy children. The church families had children and teens and the church naturally developed into a balanced, close-knit family. Sis. Testerman wrote and directed Christian plays for the youth group and we had meaningful holiday celebrations. Sunday School, Vacation Bible Schools, baptisms, and revivals. God was forming His church.

My school friends started attending like the Smith twins, Marilyn and Carolyn, with their siblings and parents. The whole family was talented. I participated in the church choir and youth meetings. My siblings thought I was a little strange because I didn't even want to miss business meetings!

My brother got married there to a girl in the church right after graduation, Nell Testerman, and my sister Carolyn got married there to Hubert Croslin and then finished high school. Other weddings, funerals, baby dedications, birthdays, and special events were part of the church family. God the Father chooses us, Christ the Son saves us, Holy Spirit seals us, and we are adopted children and heirs. We became a family. The church is not LIKE a family. It IS a family.

One summer when I was seventeen, I got a job at an engineer's office, but I had to miss youth camp at the First Mission Camp Ground. The first one I missed since I was a child. But I promised to go to the last night and pick up the campers and distribute them to their homes in Owasso.

Friday afternoon I arrived at the camp in time to go with the girls to the traditional prayer grove service. Something I had done many times before. I could feel the excitement of the last night of camp with the exchanges of phone numbers and addresses of new and old friends.

The music of the last day of camp is always heartfelt in a special way and usually enthusiastically loud. The last sermon was a challenge to surrender and serve God with all your might.

Midnight Call

After good-byes and tearful hugs, we loaded up campers and bags. It was late by the time I delivered campers to their thankful parents. I quickly read a scripture and knelt by my bed for a short prayer of thanks. As I crawled into my bed, the words of the evangelist entered my mind. Was I willing to surrender all to serve God with all my might? I had done so before, yes. The thought came like a light on my forehead. I AM TO BE A MISSIONARY.

I crawled out of bed and knelt again.

"What? I have been saying since a child, I was surrendered. Why did you wait so long? What about my scholastic scholarship to college? What about my boyfriend? How can we afford for me to study at Bible College to prepare?"

I lay back under the sheet. I AM TO BE A MISSIONARY.

Again, on my knees I tearfully and joyfully said, "Okay, Lord. I will. I want to. I want to!"

"Trust in the Lord will all your heart, and lean not on your own understanding. In all your ways acknowledge Him, and He will direct your paths." Proverbs 3:5, 6. This promise still brings direction to me in my Winter Season.

Surprisingly I went to sleep after trying to imagine how I would break the news to my folks.

The next day I was riding between my two parents in the solid front seat of their Buick. I explained the conversation I had with the Lord and that I wouldn't be applying at OU but would need to go to Welch College (then FWBBC) in Nashville, Tennessee.

I remember that we were crossing over old Bird Creek Bridge. They were silent for a few seconds.

Mother said, "We have known since you were nine years old that you would be called to ministry. You even said as a little girl that you wanted to be a missionary. I have hidden it in my heart."

We were both tearful by then.

My Father spoke up, "Don't worry about your school. We will do what we can to help you. God will provide."

Bird Creek has a new bridge now and it is named after him, "Rev. W.T. 'Tommy' Roberts" in honor of his developing the town with his buildings and streets, and founding the church that now has a Christian School, a large congregation on a beautiful campus, and a church family that makes a difference in the community. Thank you, nephew, State Representative Eric Proctor. But I remember each time I cross the bridge of that conversation with my folks and with the Lord.

I had to cut my heart strings with my boyfriend that night. That was very difficult for my young heart. I leaned against the door after he left and cried until I couldn't anymore and then peace, sweet peace came. We both found Christian mates and have been happy. I have never doubted my calling and I can declare that He is faithful until now, in my Winter Time Season.

Graduation Night Surprise.

In 1960 our senior class at Owasso High School had rented an electric organ for our graduation ceremony, invited a speaker, invited family and friends, prepared our caps and gowns and were ready to celebrate. About 35 of us had successfully finished our four years with the help of a dedicated group of faculty and staff and the support of our families.

However, our plans were quickly changed. A tornado took out all electrical power! The whole city was in the dark. We were a close-knit group so we put our heads together to decide what to do next. Go ahead with graduation or go home?

Typical of our group, we decided to gather from florist shops and funeral homes candelabras to light up the gymnasium. We were thankful to Scotty Glasgow, James Neal and the many others who braved the wind and rain at its peak to gather up enough candles and candelabras to light the gym for the evening. The piano was brought out for our music in place of the rented organ. Mr. Ed Flynn, organist, played both the processional and recessional on the piano as if it were in our original plans!

Rev. Bascom Doak gave the invocation and Rev. Ray Be bout the benediction. I was fortunate to have some Christian friends in my graduating class who attended church with me. Two dear Christian's friends who were not of my church were mentioned in the program that night.

Our Salutatorian was my friend Robert Thiessen, an active member of the Mennonite Brethren Church and a good example of a Christian young man. He had a grade average of 3.75. He had attended school in Owasso all of his 12 school years with perfect attendance! I believe he went to OSU to major in dairy production and manufacturing.

One of my best friends was Co-Valedictorian with me, Janet Streeter. She had a grade average of 4.0. She attended the Methodist Church and was president of the MYF. She started school at Owasso in 1958.

I moved to Owasso in 1957 when I was a sophomore. As I told you, I really enjoyed school. Even after attending six schools in six different cities, I had a grade average of 4.0 for my entire 12 years of school. Only by the grace of God, encouragement by my parents, and lots of study hours!

I was chosen to be the student speaker for the night, but the stage was dark! I could not read the notes I had made and had rehearsed for my speech, so I just spoke from my heart to my dear classmates and our families. I don't remember much of the speech, but I commented that one day we might pass through doors in the market places and run on to each other. Actually, after I left and went on to college and then to the mission field in Brazil, it was 50 years before we met again.

So, on that stormy Thursday night, our Superintendent Dr. Jim L. Prince and Boyd Spencer presented our diplomas and we switched our tassels. Thankful that no lives were lost in the tornado, the class of 1960 was sent off to our futures.

The local newspaper, THE OWASSON, reported May 26, 1960, "The unanimous decision to go ahead in spite of the obstacles, gave the group of graduating seniors an unusually lovely and long to be remembered commencement, and set a precedent that may be carried on (purposely, of course) by other classes in years to come."

Go Rams!

Photos of My Spring Season-USA

Marie and Tom Roberts

SHIRLEY R.

Front row:

  Wayne   Carolyn   Shirley

Back row:

  Alene   Dolores   Dean

Six Roberts Kids

Are they twins?

Shirley and Carolyn
Jefferson Grade
School in Sapulpa,
OK

Roberts Family

Dean   Alene   Dolores   Father   Mother   Wayne   Shirley
Carolyn

Will Rogers Junior High Claremore, OK 1

Owasso HS Cheer and Pep Squad - Go RAMS! 1

Homecoming Owasso High School 1

Shirley and Carolyn Jr/Sr Banquet with mom and sisters

Shirley Owasso High School Graduation

At New Home FWB church, Berryhill, Ok.

Shirley, Mother and Father

Part Two

My Summer Season

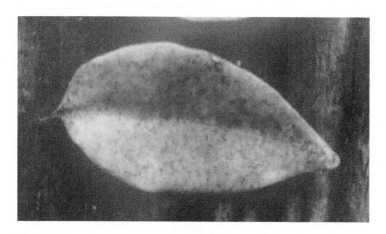

1960-2008

"Trust in the Lord with all your heart,

And lean not on your own understanding;

In all your ways acknowledge Him,

And He shall direct your paths."

Proverbs 3:5,6

Chapter Two

SUMMER SEASON BEGINS

Nashville, Tennessee

And I was soon off to Welch College (Free Will Baptist Bible College) in Nashville, Tennessee, to prepare for the amazing calling God had given to this young girl from Oklahoma. Praise God.

In preparation for my going to Bible College I started sewing some outfits for college and started saving my money. At National Association of Free Will Baptist which met in California, I went forward on the missionary challenge night to commit publicly what I had already shared with my church in Owasso, Oklahoma.

It never occurred to me to wonder if I would like the city of Nashville, Tennessee, because I knew that God was leading me and all I had to do was follow. The Lord would help with the emotions of leaving my beloved family and country.

At that time in 1960 the population of Nashville was 176, 875. That was a lot of people compared to my hometown of Owasso! It was the capital of the state and located on the Cumberland River. But, when my folks and I arrived at the campus of the College, I fell in love with the welcoming beauty of the city founded in 1779. (At the time of writing this, the population is over 695,000 and the school has changed to a nearby campus site.)

In 1942, the year I was born, the college was established and its first president, Dr. L.C. Johnson, was still president when I enrolled. He proved to be an inspirational friend, chapel speaker designed to meet personal student needs, and an example as husband and father.

Our first stop was to the administration offices on West End Avenue to talk with E.B. McDonald, the treasurer. By the time my parents finished talking with him I had a job as one of his office assistants.

I enjoyed working on the *Bulletin,* a monthly college publication to inform our denomination about the college. I enjoyed working with Mr. McDonald, the editor, and enjoyed becoming a closer friend with Nancy Combs, who became my future sister-in-law, with Jake Creech, who became a very mission minded pastor, Dale Cole, one of my dorm mates, as we worked together in the mailing room.

Our next stop was at Richland Hall, on Richland Avenue, the women's dormitory which would be my home for the next years. We were met by the Dean of Women, Mrs. J.E. Simpson who lived in the dorm with us. She was a great influence in the lives of the girls in her care. The men had three buildings as dorms and Dr. Charles A. Thigpen was Dean of Men and a professor.

We were taken to the second floor and introduced to the young women who would be my roommates. There were six of us on bunk beds in one room and the bathroom was down the hall. Freshmen young women from different states and different callings. Arkansas, California, Mississippi, North Carolina, Michigan, and Oklahoma all blended together in a way that is still in our hearts. Our prayer captain, Jean Pittman from North Carolina, was in a room nearby and helped us to understand the daily routines of campus life. They left a mark on my life.

My mother had used books of Green Stamps (remember those?) to buy items for my room and one I especially enjoyed

was a white clock radio. I had always shared items with my siblings and this was now mine alone. I had a taste of preparing for adult life apart from family. After my parents returned to Oklahoma, I had a taste of starting another chapter in my life following the Lord Jesus. Sweet and sad.

I had always enjoyed school life and was always busy. The same was true at Bible College. Work and studies took up most of our time, but in the Memorial Auditorium I experienced some of my most meaningful services in chapel, conferences, and special student body events. I met amazing denominational leaders and several missionaries preparing to go or returning from distant countries and reporting on what God is doing around the world. I was stirred and convinced that I was where God wanted me and at the time, He wanted me. But the future was still before me and I was there to prepare for that.

In the first weeks of the semester the campus started to stir with excitement among the upper classmen. It was time for Rush Week. What was that? The campus had Literary Societies for women, the Christina Rossetti Society and the Louisa Mae Alcott Society. The men's societies were the William Jennings Bryan Society and the John Bunyan Society.

Banners and posters were splashed all around campus and invitations were called out to us freshmen to join with one society or the other. I joined the Louisa Mae Alcott Literary Society whose challenge was from Ephesians 6:14, "Stand, therefore, having your loins girt bout with truth, and having on the breastplate of righteousness." I became one of the officers and enjoyed planning events and working on the society bulletin.

I came from a singing family and had been part of public school and church choirs, so it was a natural choice to be part of the college choir under our dear director, Don Clark from Oklahoma. The annual spring Choir Tour led us to other parts of the States and helped us to fellowship with many people in our denomination. A highlight.

The college placed great emphasis on prayer and missions. Missionary Prayer Band met daily to gain information and pray for world-wide missions. Miss Laura Belle Barnard, former missionary to India, was instrumental in beginning the prayer band in the early days of the college. (Once she prayed, I would have a missionary nose.) The student body was divided into six groups, each praying for a different section of the world. My vision was more opened to the importance of Bible translations and overseas Christian radio service as well as sending missionaries to other countries.

Miss Bernard was our Bible teacher and our mission's teacher. But she was so much more to me. She made us think through culture barriers, counseled us, prepared us, and spent time with us. Our love for our Lord Jesus and the Word grew and we were so ready to share its message wherever the Lord would lead.

The Foreign Mission Fellowship is a chartered chapter of Inter-Varsity Christian fellowship. The student organization was composed of members who had answered a call to international missions and associate members who were committed to being church leaders interested in promoting and supporting missions. We met weekly and sponsored semi-monthly programs.

For the ministerial students there was the Ministerial Fellowship group. For the Women there was the Woman's Auxiliary. It is now Women Active for Christ. Over fifty of us were active in the on-campus chapter. As from the beginning, this women's movement has championed children's needs, Christian education, home and international missions, and community outreach. It continues to be that today. My mother was a great promoter of this ministry, state president in California, so it was natural for me to want to be an active member in college.

Jim, At First sight

Whew, I was busy! But I was not so busy that I did not notice one young ministerial student. His name was Jim. He was an officer in several groups, class president, worked on the yearbook, in the choir, with a 4.0 average, studying for the ministry...but not a missionary candidate! I noticed other young men who were dedicated, and handsome, but they were not missionary candidates either!

Every meal, except Friday nights, the students were assigned to a certain table in the cafeteria in order to get acquainted with more classmates. . They would change often, so it really worked. Once, I was assigned to the same table as the young man I had been admiring. I learned that his father was a Free Will Baptist pastor, he was from a family of 15 children by one mother, had already been in the navy, and he had a girlfriend.

Even being a pastor's son, Jim had not accepted Christ as Lord and Savior of his life when he signed up for the Navy at 17 years old. He and his friend, Patrick, had talked about surrendering to Christ when they were older.

One day on the ship, Jim received a letter and a news clipping from his mother. He read that Patrick had drowned while on a fishing trip with Jim's father and brother. He was in shock with the news, but his first thought was whether Patrick was prepared to meet God. He broke down and accepted Christ right there on the ship.

He said while he was working in the ship's radar section, he had time to read a Bible he had taken with him. During that time, he felt God was calling him to preach. So, he was at Bible College to prepare for the ministry – not missions!

Each year the school's Missions Conference was a great blessing to me and others. At the end of an evening service, a young couple and others went forward to surrender to missionary service. It was the response we had prayed for. Well, the couple turned out to be Jim and his girlfriend.

School studies and activities continued and God continued to prepare us for our futures. I had joined the Louisa Mae Alcott Literary Society and we were rehearsing a Shakespearean comedy with the John Bunyan Literary Society. News got around at rehearsal that Jim and his girlfriend weren't dating anymore. So, to my surprise, as I was placing the gestors collar on Jim, he teased a little and then asked me to sit with him for

Friday night hotdogs. I accepted and we had several Friday night hot-dog dates.

In spite of the "six-inch-rule", no contact between dating couples, and the fact that he was pastoring a country church on Sundays and we couldn't "walk around the block" as other couples did, we spent the rest of semester getting acquainted. I didn't have any trouble accepting the rules because I knew I was where God wanted me.

Several couples had dated under those rules and many have great marriages. We discovered many things in common and many things different. A mixture God was going to combine for His glory.

I remember one incident, though. Choir was one of the highlights of our year under the direction of dear Dr. Don Clark. On a Choir tour bus, we were allowed to sit by each other. Jim reached for my hand under a pillow and squeezed it. We had never touched and it sent a tingle up my arm and to my heart. But, at the same time I was surprised and hoped no one had seen it. I didn't need to worry. Jim went to Bro Thigpen, the Dean of Students, and confessed! I was actually relieved and proud of him, but I still remembered the tingle. On that trip he told me he had already bought an engagement ring but since students weren't allowed to get engaged during the school semester, he couldn't show it to me.

The Tumble

One sunny winter afternoon near the end of the semester, I was leaving the upstairs library of the Alumni Building at closing time. The metal fire escape stairs were closer to our dorms than the front entrance, but I had not counted on a little ice left on the cold metal. My shoe soles slipped and since my arms were around my text books I had been studying, I didn't catch myself. I slid down the cold stairs on my back hitting each step until I didn't remember anything.

At the bottom of the stairs, I couldn't seem to open my eyes at first, but I sensed people around me talking. I recognized the voice of Mr. Tommy Burch, my social studies professor (one of my favorite subjects) and I was not only feeling pain, but for some reason I was embarrassed to open my eyes. I was finally helped up and taken to the dorm.

Someone called my parents after the doctor said I needed complete rest. They had moved from Oklahoma to Kansas to pastor a church there. When my parents arrived, the doctor had prescribed pain medicine that made me feel like I was in a back room observing everything. Strange. I had only one more semester test to take for a night class and I didn't want to lose those credits. But the medicine still kept me like I was in a trance.

The night of the test I showed up, but I hardly remembered completing it. But one thing I do remember. I made the first "C" grade in my life!

Jim was completing his degree in three and a half years at the top of his class. He was leaving to pastor a church in Franklin, Ohio and my parents were going to take me to their home in Shawnee Mission, Kansas, where my father was pastor.

It was the last night of the school session. I didn't know it, but Jim had asked permission from Bro. Thigpen to give me my ring before he left to go to Ohio and I to Oklahoma. Under the dim light of the front steps of the auditorium with students all around, he reached for my hand slipped the ring on my finger. But it was the wrong finger and it wouldn't slip on! He was nervous and I was nervous, but he found the correct finger and the commitment was made. He whispered he would seal the deal with a kiss later. We had set the wedding date for May 4th so we had about four months before we would see each other again. Before I could collect that kiss.

He had been invited to pastor a church in Franklin, Ohio where our friends Richard, Lurlie, and Valetta Howard attended.

Shawnee Mission, Kansas and the Wedding

My father was building the church parsonage so they were temporarily renting a house. It was there that I wrote letters to Jim every day and I received one from him every day from Ohio. During the next 53 years Jim rarely gave me cards for Mother's Day, Birthdays, or Valentine's Day and even fewer letters or phone calls. I had about 150 letters saved from him, though, that kept me encouraged to prepare for our wedding.

A fine, Christian chiropractor from Kansas City started treatments and I was soon better. However, after examination, he said that I might have trouble giving birth. He was already a friend to my parents, but he couldn't attend the wedding. We had never worked with tape recorders before, but he promised to record our wedding as a present. A new idea to us.

The beautiful parsonage was finished and we moved into another lovely home my father built.

The church was new to me and I enjoyed meeting so many wonderful people. As usual, my father invited all missionaries passing through Kansas to the church so I got better acquainted with several. I started singing solos again before my father's sermons. Sometimes, he would call me up at the last minute. Just like old times.

I learned so much while I was there those months from watching my mother love and serve the church. I knew I would be a pastor's wife in the church in Ohio and I wanted to learn so much. The International Mission Board required ministry experience before going to the mission field. Jim was already a pastor and we had both grown up in pastors' homes, but we had never done ministry together. I was hoping we would have a lifetime to do that somewhere in God's leading.

The first week of May finally arrived. Two days before Jim was expected to arrive, I was mopping the floors and helping to prepare the house for the arrival of his family from different states and for my family from Oklahoma. Surprise! When I looked up from my mop bucket, there was my handsome groom to be. I felt like I was a mess, but I was soon in his arms and finally got the promised kiss.

The parsonage had a large basement and we had prepared several double beds for out-of-town relatives. The Friday night before the wedding on Saturday the guests had arrived. My sister, Dolores, had made me a beautiful white lace wedding gown and brought it to me from Oklahoma. It fit perfectly. I had chosen my wedding bouquet of roses and lilies. The names of Jesus my Lord. "The Rose of Sharon and The Lilly of the Valley." They were to be picked up the day of the wedding. The ladies of the church were helping with the reception after the church wedding.

The next morning my mother had prepared a big breakfast for over 30 people. A lady from the church had given me a permanent and my long hair was gone! Oh, well. Nothing was going to ruin my joy that day.

Bride-napped

Well, something happened that took the joy from my sisters, Dean, Dolores, and Alene, for a while. Three of my four brothers–in-law present, "bride-napped" me for a joyride. I have loved all of them since I was young so it was all in fun.

They took me all around Kansas City. At the first stop they bought me a long, plastic bat to use on my new husband, they said. Then they bought us all popcorn. The way they started whispering, I guessed they were lost in the city.

They stopped at a service station and I saw a phone booth. I ran and phoned my family. They said my sisters were so nervous and upset with their husbands and one sister had already fainted. Oh, dear. It was really getting late. I had a wedding to go to! Did someone go after the flowers?

The guys were getting a little nervous, too, but finally found their way back to Shawnee Mission and delivered the bride. They were in trouble, but I had to get ready for my wedding in just a short time.

It started raining. To me it was a good sign. It was snowing when I was born. It rained, a tornado, actually, at my high school graduation. It rained when I went to Nashville. All good memories with rain. As my story develops, God sent more rainy days.

My father performed the ceremony. Jim's father said the prayer. My younger sister, Carolyn, and niece, Sharron, were the matrons of honor. My little nieces, Deborah, Dianne, and Rhonda, and little nephews, Danny and Raymond were all included to take care of the flowers and rings. All so beautiful in their special made wedding clothes. I loved my family and would soon be moving far from them, so it was a joy to have them to be part of my wedding.

My family, Jim's family, and church people were all there from different states. My high school best friends, Rick and Carolyn Dossett were there from Owasso, Oklahoma. Our college friend from West Virginia, Jim Sturgill, was our photographer. Black and white photos at that time. Ten years later a flood in our city of Tubarao swept away the album, but I was given some copies my parents had. Memories are filed in our head, but photos certainly help.

Jim had borrowed a car from the Howards in Ohio and we left out in it that rainy Saturday night. He had already made reservations in a motel in Kansas City, The Pink Pelican. All these years the sight of pink pelicans remind of our wedding night.

The next morning, we looked up a Baptist Church close by to go to our first church service together as a married couple, before starting out for Franklin, Ohio, and the next chapter in our lives. We stopped one more night before arriving at the parsonage of the church in Ohio.

Franklin, Ohio Experience

The church parsonage was a three-level home next to the church. Since we were going to Brazil after a year at the church, we didn't bother with furniture. They had a bed in one of the bedrooms, and a table and chairs in the kitchen. The chair bottoms were of cloth and someone suggested we just paint a layer of varnish on them and they would look new again. They were right! The house had many built-in closets and cabinets so we were fine.

I fell in love with the people of the church. I especially loved to work with the youth and women. The songs were the same as our home churches in Oklahoma and West Virginia. They had invitations and altar services, and united prayer at the altar just like I had grown up with. They were so open to mission work and community outreach. We had learned that you observe the gifts of the members and not change anything too quickly. There was nothing to change. Just to add our time and gifts to theirs to grow spiritually together. The Howard family was very helpful and became as family.

We made a quick trip back to Nashville for Jim to walk across the stage with his graduation class of 1963. . He was one of the top scholars and top in my heart. I was a proud wife.

We had many learning experiences that year in Franklin. I believe that we were paid $45.00 and the church furnished a house and utilities. So, when Jim was asked to drive a bus for a handicapped children's school, he accepted. I was asked to substitute teach second graders at the local public school for a teacher on leave and I accepted. We not only invested in the children, but we made friends with several families. Both were great experiences and big adventures!

The International Missions headquarters had asked us to pray about a field of service. I had had several contacts with young

Mexicans visiting the church my father pastored, and Jim was interested in Africa. A missionary from Brazil, Ken Eagleton visited our church in Franklin and stayed with us in the parsonage. We talked until late and he challenged us to pray about going to Brazil. He shared that over half of the population at that time was of youth and children. People did have Bibles but they did not read them. At that time the priest taught it was dangerous to study the Bible without the guidance of a priest.

I searched information about Brazil in the encyclopedias and National Geographic magazines. We read about the mission work there by Free Will Baptists.

When the year at the church ended, we moved into a little one room apartment at the back of the Howard's house. And then we went on the road.

On The Many Roads

We visited our headquarters in Nashville to finish our applications for overseas service.

At our last meeting with the mission board, we had all committed to pray for God's leading about to what country we were to go. We already knew that several of our classmates had gone to Ivory Coast, Africa and the board members were looking to other fields. Perhaps Ecuador for one. Jim and I had peace in suggesting Brazil.

At the meeting, the board had dismissed the possibility of opening Ecuador at the time. They had a suggestion. Brazil. At that time, we shared that we were considering it, also. Brazil. We felt God had confirmed a country for us. Out of many countries, groups of people, and types of ministries, the one HE chose was fine with us. Brazil.

Now to make contacts, share that Jesus said to go into all the world and that each Christian could be part of what God wants to do to win the lost. Some of those in the pews and homes needed to go. Some needed to send us and others. We were ready.

Since my father had been a pastor in the states of Oklahoma, Kansas, and California and Jim's father had been a pastor in the states of West Virginia, Georgia and Florida, with so many contacts we had raised support quickly. It was by God's grace. Since we didn't have children, we scheduled two services on Sundays, a service on Wednesday nights, District meeting, women's meetings, men's meetings, youth camps, Bible colleges, and Sunday Schools. We traveled from Florida to California, Michigan to Texas, and all between. At that time, month long state wide missions' conferences were scheduled. We were there.

Like the example in the Bible, we were commissioned with the laying on of hands at the Kilsyth Free Will Baptist Church in Mount Hope, West Virginia. Then at my home church in Owasso, Oklahoma, Jim and I knelt before the church and they laid hands on us and sent us off.

Send Off Good-byes

Support was raised and promised by our senders. The capable mission personnel helped us with documents necessary, enrollment in language school, airline tickets, and orientation. Many people were praying.

I hit one bump when I went to get my Passport. I have shared how I was not registered as an infant because there was no doctor present on that snowy, stormy night. I had no birth certificate. When I went to get my driver's license, the policeman accepted the registration in the Family Bible. But no way would the government accept the Family Bible. We got busy and with the testimony of my oldest sister and a little more red tape I had my birth certificate.

With all the preparation and prayer, we still had to face the moment to say good-bye to our families for five years. Back then in 1964, the first terms, because of the first year of language study, were five years instead of four. Our young niece Sharron Annette gave me a five-year diary which was filled by the time we returned home and saw her again.

One great blessing was that our parents encouraged us and had really prepared us spiritually for that day in December. We left my family in Tulsa, Oklahoma, and we packed my parents' car and they went with us to Florida where we would meet Jim's parents who were there pastoring a church. Our flight was to leave from Miami.

At the airport, with our parents and relatives praying for our trip, we said our good-byes. As parents, they understood better than we just how long five years would be and how much life would happen while we were apart.

Flying on the same plane with us were Don and Carol Robirds and their children. They were from California and from the church my father pastored.

At that time, our planes stopped in Panama City and Quito, Ecuador. I learned to pack better after that first trip.

In Quito there was a cardboard box that burst open at the foot of the steps going into the plane. A man was watching to see if someone identified the contents. Well, a lace nighty was lying on the ground that looked very familiar. Embarrassing! Yes, we found out the hard way how weak tape and twine are in the hands of baggage handlers.

Chapter Three

FIRST TERM BEGINS - 1964

Campinas, Brazil- Arrival

Our plane arrived at the *Vira Copos Aeroporto Internacional* in Campinas, Sao Paulo, in December of 1964. It was a hot, hot summer in December, but it was raining that special day.

Missionaries were at the airport with their vehicles to meet the Robirds and us and to help with the baggage. We were taken to the house of Missionaries Earnie and Willie Jean Deeds, and their children, Lyndon and Ladonna. Earnie and Willie Jean had just finished language school and he was pastoring the local church in Campinas. The very first church of our mission in Brazil.

Other missionary families were at the Deeds' house to welcome us. Brazil was a new field at that time and they tried to all get together to welcome new missionaries. Already serving in Brazil when the Robirds and we arrived were Bobby and Sue Aycock, Sam and June Wilkinson, Bobby and Geneva Poole, Walter and Marcia Ellison. Ken and Marvis Eagleton. Two single missionaries were Eula Mae Martin, a nurse, and Mary Ellen Rice, in Child Evangelism. Dave Franks was our first missionary appointed to Brazil. He came single, but after furlough he brought back a nurse, Pat Sturgill Franks, from West Virginia as his wife.

I happened to arrive not feeling well and tried not to show it. Since we were newlyweds of one year, some of the women started asking questions and teasing that maybe we were expecting a child. We weren't, but we were before the year of language school was finished.

A house was rented on Rua Orlando Caprine in the Castelo Branco neighborhood in Campinas. The missionaries had prepared it nicely and we were able to unload our boxes and barrels in one of the three rooms. There was a bed for us, and later the Robirds and we would shop for the approved furniture list. A stove, refrigerator, table and four chairs, sofa and chairs. We would eventually buy our own desk and file cabinet.

We had spent months raising money to cover language school, housing, furniture, ministry expenses, and a car. The car would not be permitted until we finished language school. Meanwhile we walked or took the electric street cars.

We had a surprise when we woke up that first morning. Our bedroom was full of fleas and we were covered in bites! We heard later that the former owners had dogs in the house.

Language School

We were enrolled in the language school of *the Escola de Portugues e Orientacao* that was to begin classes in the next month. The men studied in the mornings and the women in the afternoons. That way one parent would always be free to stay with the children.

Besides the Robirds and us, Louis and Florine Coscia and Walter and Marcia Ellison from our mission were also students there. The Coscias and Ellisons were a semester ahead of us.

The language school served other missions sending missionaries to Brazil. The teachers were Brazilians who spoke NO English to us. The teaching method was based on the fact that children in their cribs can speak in sentences without ever reading or writing. With that method, we learned that we had to humble ourselves as little children in order to survive five days a week of drilling repetition.

One phrase was *"Gostou do frango frito?" "Gostou do frango frito?" Gostou do frango fritio?"* I wondered if I could greet folks on the street car or my neighbors with this phrase. What was I saying?

For 15 days we repeated what we thought we heard and were corrected. Repeated again and then corrected. We saw nothing written in Portuguese or English. Just repeated, repeated. After two weeks the professors must have been pleased with our pronunciation because they handed out papers with the meanings in English. No Portuguese, yet.

Well, it is a good thing I didn't' use *"Gostou do frango frito?"* It means "Did you like the fried chicken?"!!

I kept a little pocket dictionary to help me write down new vocabulary. At least what it sounded like to me. But one day I learned a new word the hard way.

The Peddler

It was common for vendors to pass by our little rent house peddling raw milk (which we had to boil), and fruits and vegetables. One morning while Jim was in class, I was home alone and heard a clap at our gate. I was curious to see who was there, but knew I couldn't communicate very well. Standing by the gate was a short, smiling man holding the handles of a wheel barrow that was covered with an old tarp.

He started talking in Portuguese to me and I was pretty sure he was giving a sales pitch, but I didn't understand a word and I wanted to take a peek under the tarp. We weren't getting anywhere.

I took out the dictionary and looked up the word *comer.*

"Senhor, comer?"

I repeated my question, *"Comer?"*

He looked shocked.

He repeated the word, *"Comer? Nao, nao, nao, Senhora!"*

He threw up his hands and started rattling more Portuguese as he pushed his wheel barrow on down the street. Wow. I didn't know if I had offended him and just stood there watching as he continued on shaking his head.

When Jim returned home, I told him about our visitor at the gate. I couldn't understand Portuguese enough to search for a Portuguese word in the dictionary and Jim didn't have an idea about what had happened.

At language school that afternoon, I shared my story with other missionaries. The Ellisons, Coscias, and Robirds from our mission were also studying there. The Ellisons lived on the same street as we, and the man had also passed by their house. When the ladies heard my tale, they looked at each other and burst out laughing.

"Shirley, the man had *esterco* under the tarp."

The other missionaries who were in more advanced classes had understood and started laughing.

"Okay. *Esterco,* so it must not be something to eat?"

"No, Shirley, *esterco* means fertilizer – animal manure."

Oh, dear. Well, that was one more new word for my growing vocabulary list.

Flannel Graph Helpers

Before going to Brazil, I had never taught English as a second language, but we soon found out that it opened many doors to make contacts and to share the Good News.

While we were still living in our little rent house during language school in Campinas, two young women were clapping at out gate. Who could that be? We hardly knew anyone except our Brazilian teachers and other missionaries in the school.

We invited them into our sparsely furnished living room – a sofa, two chairs, and overturned cardboard packing boxes covered with towels from the mission Provision closet. Well, they sort of looked like end tables.

The young ladies weren't looking at the furniture; they were looking at us with young shiny eyes. They were speaking broken English, but we understood they were asking for

English classes. They were in college and English was a required subject for them.

I explained that I studied Portuguese in the language school each afternoon, and if they wanted English classes studying the Bible with flannel graph figures, I would try to find time for classes for them. (I still had the flannel graph figures packed somewhere, didn't I?)

The girls worked Monday through Friday and studied at the university at night. After several attempts and lots of laughs, we finally understood each other enough to schedule classes each Saturday morning.

We were renting a tiny two-bedroom house, so we hurriedly made a desk out of some planks of boards over packing barrels and placed three of our four Formica kitchen chairs in the empty front bedroom for the classes.

I found the box of flannel graph Bible figures and wrapped a flannel gown around plywood to use as my board. I decided to start with Genesis since there was great vocabulary in those first chapters. I was ready for my first experience in teaching English as a second language. They were ready for their first experience of studying God's Word in a second language.

About thirty years later I offered free adult conversational English classes called "The Gospel of Love". I got out the flannel graph figures again and taught the Gospel of John to professional people, business people, and government workers. It gave the same satisfaction of dividing the word with people who, for the most part, had never heard it before.

Eventually we became fluent in Portuguese and would teach the precious Word for over forty-four years in Brazil in both languages. However, teaching the Bible in English as a second language to two young women who clapped at our gate each Saturday morning is one of the most precious memories I have of that time.

While still in language school we learned that it is not enough to learn the language, you need to understand the culture. When you preach about being "born again", some think you are teaching reincarnation. When you teach it is good for Christians to marry, but it is good to be single, too, they interpret that they can live together without marrying.

The first barriers that sometimes need to be broken when you evangelize in a foreign country are language, culture, and their past experiences. Sometimes it is a tough, time consuming job of love and persistence. Then the Holy Spirit takes over and breaks through.

Before leaving language school, we met missionaries from the Unevangelized Field Missions (UFM) who were taking a refresher course in Portuguese. They worked in the jungles of the *Territorial de Roraima*. I remember thinking, "Now, they are real missionaries." They returned after language study to their compound in the jungles and they invited us to visit them, which we did at the end of our first five-year term. You will meet them in another chapter of this book.

After a year of studies, five days a week, of persistent study and prayer, you feel you can talk 'baby talk" in your adopted language. By the day of our graduation in December of 1965,

I was five months along in expecting our first child. I had been chosen to give the speech to the graduating class and faculty and friends. In Portuguese. Pressure?

I whispered to our director sitting by me on the stage,

"Acho que vou desmaiar".

He whispered back, "Oh, no. You can't faint at this late date. You will do fine."

My teachers had drilled me on the pronunciation of the scriptures I was to read and on my short comments. I felt so much more than I could express in that language that day. It was a foundation, though, that I could build on to share the truth and hope in Jesus Christ for the last sixty years.

Araras, Sao Paulo – First house,

We had visited with Bobby and Sue Aycock in Araras, about an hour north of Campinas. They had started working with a group of new converts and Jim and I were there for the organization of the church. They were meeting in a small rented one room building on one of the main streets downtown.

Their house was just a block away and they were leaving to return to the United States for their state-side assignment. The field council of all the resident missionaries had asked us to go there to assume the ministry. So, we moved into their house on *Rau Tridents, 39.*

Remember, we had just left language school able to speak the very basic vocabulary and phrases. But with faith that God had put us with the small group of new converts, and a lot of writing out lessons and messages, Jim assumed the preaching and a 30-minute radio program on Friday nights. I taught the youth in Sunday School and shared with the children and women. They were so patient and we just laughed our way through the first months. Our weaknesses were a bonding time with those precious people. They were falling in love with Jesus and we were falling in love with them.

Another bonding factor was that I was in my fifth month of expecting our first child. Often, they would say that we were *marinheiros na primeira viagem.* Sailors on our first journey.

Plant a Church, Friendship Evangelism

In the small rented building on Tiradente Street, we had about a dozen people. But with Sunday School and preaching each Sunday morning and night we saw people timidly enter our store front church and then respond to the gospel.

Jim had a radio program Friday night for 30 minutes titled, "Palavra da Esperanca." Word of Hope. We offered free Bibles, counseling, and invitations to our Bible studies. Some responded.

Some came after studying English and were curious to know more. That opened doors to friendship with the Fachini family. Two of their sons became missionaries. One was a missionary pilot in the Amazon jungle.

A business lady, Antonia, accepted a gospel tract from a market in town owned by a church member, Odete. She found courage to go to a Bible study, in spite of her family and local priest. She found the truth she was looking for and her children, William, Rita, and Emerson, also. They were all baptized and active in the church. One grandson, Jefferson, is a missionary pilot in the Amazon.

In *Escola Biblica de Ferias, Vacation Bible School,* many children came. We loved on them and made contacts with their families. Two little sisters attended one year and one, Rejeane, accepted Jesus as Savior. She later married Kenneth Eagleton, son of missionaries Ken and Marvis, and they took four sons to Ivory Coast where they were missionaries and then to Brazil. Rejeane's mother attended the church, too.

Araras – First Baby

While in language school in Campinas we discovered that I was expecting, and a local Christian doctor was recommended for my pre-natal visits. Then when we moved to Araras, a lady from our tiny church group recommended her doctor to me. Dr. Enio was highly esteemed in the town.

Oops! On my first visit to this office, I realized that I couldn't understand him. He spoke Portuguese at a very, very fast pace. He was quite attentive and explained many things, but even with a dictionary in my hand I couldn't keep up. Yes, I felt like a sailor on my first journey and my boat was getting rocky.

I was continents away from my mother and four sisters and there were no other Americans in town. That vocabulary he was using had not been taught at language school and I was really lost. You can believe that I spent time trying to learn it.

After hearing the phrase many times, *quando a fruto for madura, caira' (when* the fruit is ripe, it will fall), my contractions with the baby began. About five minutes apart. Jim checked me into the hospital that Monday in 1966, and we were so excited. My doctor looked in on us in the room that night and left me in the hands of the Catholic nuns who ran the hospital.

All night the nuns did the "toque" but said there was no dilation. That's right, no dilation, but the pains were still five minutes apart. They called a young intern to check on me, Nelson Salome'. He continued to check on me day and night.

The next day my friend from the church, Odete Cressoni, visited me and saw my situation. She explained, in slow Portuguese, that my doctor had to leave town and the Catholic nuns at that time did not believe in Caesarean-section birth.

She said, "This is the type of pain that you don't want to go away or to diminish. You want it to get harder and harder because you are going to have a baby in your arms pretty soon. Then it will be worth it all. "

The Bible says something similar, and she was right. But there was one more night and one more day of pain.

All day and all night my pains continued, and my water broke.

They prepared me for the birth, and Dr. Nelson continued to check on me. My doctor needed to return soon!

I held onto the old-fashioned iron hospital head posts as the pains continued. I heard moans and screams from the other rooms, but I was determined not to join their choir. My poor husband was sympathetic, but at times he just had to leave the room. He was a sailor on his first journey as a father, but he didn't have an iron post to hold on to with each pain. There was one more night of pain.

The next day, Wednesday, April 20, my doctor returned.

He entered into my room and said, "Okay, Dona Shirley, what is it? A boy or a girl?"

"I don't know doctor. I haven't had my baby yet, but my water already broke."

He sped out of the room. Immediately there were uniformed nuns in my room rolling me out into the hallway. Soon Jim was walking beside my roiling bed looking down at me. He kissed me on the forehead and said he was praying.

They gave me a type of spinal tap and I was aware of those in the room – my own Dr. Enio, young Dr. Nelson, and missionary nurse Eula Mae Martin who had driven down from Ribeirao Preto to be with me. She could speak perfect Portuguese and was a help to Jim.

Yes, soon I had our own little son in my arms, and, yes, it was worth it. He was so pink and with just a little fuzz of silver white hair. Since he was so different from the other babies that day, the nursery workers carried the little gringo around to show to others. (Most of the other babies had hair – dark hair.)

Welcome, Kemper Jonathan Combs. His great grandmother, Mamaw Combs, named him Kemper before I was even expecting. Since it was also my husband's name, it was a good choice. Searching for a Bible name, we considered two men in the Bible that had a good solid record. It was between Jonathan and Daniel. We decided on Jonathan. So, Kemper Jonathan Combs is the name of our first born.

Nurse Eula Mae talked to the doctor about circumcising the baby before we went home. The doctor explained,

"In Brazil it is not our custom to do that to an infant. We wait until the child is older and if an infection appears, we can do surgery".

Eula Mae politely said, "Okay. We feel it is less painful to do it as an infant as the custom is explained in the Bible. We have a Christian doctor in Campinas who understands this. We can take little Kemper there."

Dr. Enio thought a moment and then said, "Okay. We will do the circumcision here as you suggest."

Thank you, Dr. Enio.

We took our first born to the *Araras Igreja Batista Livre* church for his dedication to the Lord.

Second house, Useful Garage

When Kemper was about one year old, we moved to *Rua Alfredo Martienzi*. It was an older house and the kitchen was not sealed. We could see the red roof tiles but it did not leak. The ashes from the burning sugar cane drifted into town, however, and into our kitchen and on our laundry hanging on the backyard lines.

But it had trees around it which we enjoyed, and an old detached garage. Jim remodeled the garage with book shelves for evangelical material to help new believers. It was a cross between a lending library and bookstore and we allowed folks to enter and browse.

Interesting, but our interest in discipleship included written material to help with spiritual growth. Much of it we had to write and prepare ourselves, but there were still good offers for Bibles, study helps, and gospel music. Later we opened the first Christian book store in Araras right downtown on Tiradentes Street. It was called LER (Livraria Evangelica Rochedo). We also sold office and school supplies which brought customers who were curious about some of the materials. That opened up opportunities to share the gospel. One of my favorite customers was a Catholic nun who worked with children. I supplied her with visuals, children's music, and lots of ideas.

We were able to offer employment to a lady from our church, Zoraide. In each project we must include the national Christians from the beginning. In the weekly radio programs, we included young men from the church and musicians to lead in the services. We wrote and prepared material for VBS and trained the workers to teach the lessons and to plan the songs and scriptures. Things that would have been easier and faster if we had done them ourselves. But it was their country and their challenge to win the souls.

In other words, the missionaries must work themselves out of a job. Right from the start, like us.

Buy land, Provide a Permanent Meeting Place

On the south side of town in empty pasture land, the group bought some land and started to build a permanent church building on *Rua 13 de Maio*. Water had not reached there since there were no residents nearby. We bought kilometers of water hoses to pass water to the work site. Since Brazilian structures are based on brick and mortar, water was very important to that construction.

Many souls surrendered to salvation in Jesus Christ in that building. A safe place for courageous people to leave their old lives and face family and culture resistance.

Many were trained and discipled there. Much music was made to the glory and worship of our Lord. Weddings were performed for couples in that building. Infants were dedicated. Christian's lives were celebrated before their bodies were taken to the cemetery.

Soon Jim had an outdoor brick water tank in front of the church with steps leading down into it. Our baptistery! Many people entered the waters from obedient baptism.

The mission strategy was to plant churches about 100 kilometers for the next church so as to have fellowship and partnership with others. The existing churches met annually on Good Friday, a holiday in Brazil, and one year they arrived in buses to meet together at our church in Araras. Other years the buses went to *Evangelandia,* the mission camp grounds. God was building His church in that country.

The Demons Talked

Mission classes in Bible College and orientation classes in language school did not prepare us for dealing with demon-possessed victims. Jim and I both grew up in pastors' homes and we had experienced pastoring a church together, but nothing prepared for me the scenes I saw many times of victims being thrown on the ground by evil spirits at the sound of the name and blood of Jesus Christ. Of hearing for the first time the voice of demons speaking through the voice boxes of tormented victims.

My books have reported many of those incidents of victory by singing about the blood and name of Jesus, about reading scriptures from the Word of God in the presence of demons. But I want to share examples with you. You can read about more in my other books.

Of course, we knew that when Lucifer rebelled in heaven from pride that God cast him out and many angels went with him. Lucifer, Satan, and the fallen angels, demons, are at war against God's plan to redeem mankind. But I never thought I would hear their voices. See their tormented victims.

But the most impressive memory was the power of even the mention of the name and blood of Jesus, the Son of God. The church learned to start singing about the blood when someone dropped into the aisle manifesting an evil spirit. We saw the demon's reactions when certain scriptures were read in their presence.

These examples I share are not to show the ugliness of the powers of darkness, but to show the mighty power and victory of Christ over darkness.

Legion

My first experience of that victory was at a conference in the Araras church. During the sermon of a visiting pastor, a lady fell out onto the floor. The church, after adjusting to the commotion, started singing. "*Ha poder, sim, forca sem igual so no sangue de Jesus?*" I felt chills as the group sang the words to "There is Power in the Blood." I was learning something so new to me as I observed and participated.

She was a small woman but it took four men to carry her weight into a classroom at the back. That was true of all the cases I knew and heard about. A spirit possessed person is heavier than his or her natural weight. She looked unconscious.

In the classroom, they placed the woman seated in a chair in the middle of the room. Her eyes were closed and her head was dropped down with her chin resting on her chest. (I was just glad she didn't slide out of her chair.) I was seated with others in chairs against the wall in front of her.

The men started praying in the name of Jesus and by the power of His blood. They read scripture about the name and blood of Jesus. The battle had begun. What a battle!

While the woman was in the trance with her eyes closed, the pastor started asking questions. The rest in the room were praying.

"How long have you been in her body?" he asked.

A low raspy voice came from out of her mouth. "Three months. She is good for me, and I will not let her go," the growling voice continued. He sounded like he meant business, too.

"She was not created for you but for the Holy Spirit of God." The pastor responded.

"What is your name?" (Wow! The same question Christ used in Mark 5;9, Luke 8:30)

"*Legiao.*" Legion! Her body started to jerk around in the chair. "I'll...not...let...her...go." The voice snarled. (And the same answer the demon gave.)

"In the powerful and holy name of Jesus Christ, the holy Son of God who shed His blood on the cross to save her from sins, and by His authority I command you to leave her body."

"No!" Came a grunt from her twisted mouth.

I was praying, but with my eyes open. Watch and pray. Watching the battle right before my eyes. The prayers around me got louder and the church outside the room continued to sing other songs about the name and blood of Jesus. Battle songs.

The pastor repeated, "In the name of Jesus Christ leave her body NOW. We claim her for Jesus Christ by His blood He shed on Calvary. Remember Calvary? Leave her body now and go to the place that was created for you."

Convulsions began again and an awful sound came from her mouth. Then she went limp. Her eyes remained closed but she lifted her head and slowly turned it from right to left in the direction of the door. Her eyes opened as she stared at the closed door.

"He is gone," she said in her normal, soft voice.

The praises echoed out around the room while the woman remained in her chair. She confirmed the information Legion had given and told of hideous sights and experience that she had been having.

The gospel was explained to her and she was urged to fill her life with the Holy Spirit of God through salvation. If not, the pastor warmed, the evil spirits would return.

"Oh, I don't want him to return. I want to ask Christ into my heart." "She bowed her head and repeated the sinner's prayer. This was a war and the first battle had been won. Whew!

I'll Kill Him

Another victim did not make the same choice.

One afternoon upon invitation from a lady in our church. A Brazilian evangelist went with Jim and me to her home to pray for her son. As we sat in her living room, her son and his wife were in the bedroom laughing. Cackling. Laughing non-stop. The Brazilian Christian with us said they had the 'spirit of laughter.' The mother wanted prayer for her son and asked us to wait while she called her son.

He came into the room alone. He was very cordial and we exchanged the normal ritualistic greetings. We sat down again and he sat on one end of the sofa next to me.

After we talked for a while, we read scripture with him. He was asked to read the seventh verse of the first chapter of I John. He was an educated young man and started reading. When he started to read the last part of the verse, he choked and started coughing. He asked to be excused from reading. He was encouraged to just repeat the words after the pastor but he refused. The words were "and the blood of Jesus Christ his Son cleanses us of all sin." Notice that it has the words 'blood' and 'Jesus Christ' in the same verse.

We used that verse to test if a person could read it without an evil spirit manifesting.

As we asked to be able to pray with him, he slid off the sofa and lay on his back on the floor, by my feet, with his eyes closed.

"No, don't," he muttered in a strange voice and rolled from side to side like he was struggling with someone. Another battle had begun!

We stated singing the chorus, *"O sangue de Jesus tem poder, tem poder."* The blood of Jesus has power, has power.

We stated praying again claiming the power in the Name of Jesus Christ. It never ceases to amaze me the reaction that Name causes at these times.

The spirit convulsed him and the young man started foaming at the mouth. (I remembered the same thing in Mark 9:18-20!) That was the first time I had seen that. So far, the only time. He stated growling like a dog and beating his arms against the floor.

"Don't sing *'Foi no Cruz, Foi na Cruz'* or I will kill him," threatened the growling voice.

We had not sung "At the Cross" yet but can you guess what we did just then? We didn't want the young man to get killed, but we knew he needed deliverance. When you watch a scene like that, the words you sing weigh heavily and they make a difference. To realize that demons know what we sing in church.

"I'll kill him. Don't sing *"Foi na Cruz"*, the voice snarled. The young man thrashed a while as the pastors prayed over him, battling for his soul, and we continued to pray and sing about the cross.

After he came out of his trance and they lifted him off the floor, he talked about the hideous scenes he had been seeing and of the tortuous pressure to his mind and body.

When they invited him to repent and accept Christ as Savior and the Holy Spirit to fill him, he would change the subject. He was too tired. Maybe he would some other day. They explained that salvation was the only way to keep the evil spirit from returning.

In Matthew 12:44 it says when an unclean spirit goes out of a man, he seeks a dry clean place to rest. If he finds none, he returns to the house (body) he came from and finds it all swept and in order. Then he goes and takes with him seven other spirits more wicked than himself, and they enter to live in that body!

They tried to explain this to him but he kept making excuses. They admonished him and warned him, and he finally said perhaps later.

Later didn't come and his mother said he soon became worse and he continued in his bondage, slavery and torment.

Oh, how sad to turn your back on the power of deliverance in Jesus Christ through His sacrifice one the cross. His name is above all names. There is POWER in that name. I have seen it.

Second Baby Challenge

Two years after Kemper was born in May of 1968, we had moved to *Rua Benedita Nogueira* , a dirt street near the church we had built. We were expecting our second baby. At that time there was no way to know the gender of the unborn baby.

On a Monday night I had talked Jim into going fishing with a friend at our church and he had called a young nurse from our church to sit with me.

While we were visiting, I told her I had found "spotting". She immediately made arrangements to prepare for my arrival at the hospital. Dr. Enio was my pre-natal care doctor.

It was another caesarean since, again, I had no dilation. On May 28th little Cindy Weinette Combs was born. Another little pink baby gringo with soft golden fuzz of hair. When searching for a name for her, we found Lucinda in both his family tree and my family tree. Our dear friend Sandra Cue made such a mark on us we considered the name Sandy. But in Portuguese it would be pronounced SUNDAY. So, we decided on Cindy. My only brother's name was Wayne. We chose a phonetic spelling for it, Weinette, so that it would sound good in Portuguese and English.

Dr. Enio entered my room the next day after delivering more babies. "*Bom dia*, Dona Shirley. We can circumcise your baby before you go home."

"*Obrigada, doutor*. But this time it is a baby girl."

Welcome, Cindy Weinette Combs.

And thank you Dr. Enio.

We presented our baby girl at the Araras *Igreja Batista Livre* church where her brother had been dedicated. One day we would return to that city and she would be married in that same church.

Jungle Stop Before State Side Assignment

Our five-year term was ending in 1969 and we would experience our first of many experiences of packing and storing our things for a year's absence from the ministry and from people we loved. The sweet-bitter good-byes were softened by the plans to introduce our children to our parents and siblings for the first time.

We remembered the invitation from the missionaries working in the Amazon jungle, so we had one stop before arriving in Miami, Florida. A stop that opened our eyes to the depth of God's love for all people. The naked. The savage. The tormented walking in darkness.

When we first talked with our International Mission board Brazil, we asked about jungle work. At that time Free Will Baptist had no work with the Indians, and Brazil would soon pass a law that only Brazilian missionaries would be allowed to work with the Indians.

So, our challenge was to teach the Great Commission to our young converts and let the Holy Spirit call some to the jungles of Brazil in our place. Our Brazilian FWB churches would later send Brazilian workers in to the jungles: Lelis Fachini, Juniior Travitzki, Jose' Pedro Mendes, Eliseu Cantelmo, Cecilia Virdes, and Jefferson Gaino. Today there are others in training to go as Brazilian missionaries to the unevangelized Indians.

Tiny Plane Flying into the Huge Amazon

On our way to our first stateside assignment, we flew to a simple airport in northern Brazil in the Roraima Territory at that time. There an *Asas de Socorro* pilot, Eldon Larson, flew us and our two children, Kemper and Cindy, for ten unforgettable days into the Amazon jungle.

Unforgettable also was the ride through those mountains and Amazon jungles that left me green with air sickness. But I held on because I knew we were facing the opportunity of a life time.

Our tiny plane landed on the airstrip carved out of the jungle near the mission compound. We were met by primitive Indians who wore no clothes, but wore flowers and sticks through pierced ears and noses. They gave us a curious, hands-on welcome. The missionaries were working with the Uai-Uai and Yanomami tribes. Sandra Cue and Edith Moreira were close by.

We later learned that they not only had no clothes, but they also had no spoons, salt, furniture (except for handmade hammocks), no matches nor tools and very little variety in foods or fruits. The popular Hollywood scenes of luscious fruit hanging freely all around was not typical of the Amazon around these tribes. The missionaries purposefully did not want to introduce them to many material goods to get used to, when they would not be available later. They had no notion of money, so the missionaries paid the natives who cleared out the airstrip with machetes and knives. By the way, the only time the men were required to wear loin cloths was when they worked on the airstrip. But the missionaries soon realized that they never washed their loin cloths. Stink! Stink!

They ate the monkeys and other meats they killed with their six feet long bows and poisoned tipped arrows. These were roasted on an open fire. They made cassava breads by squeezing out the poison from each manioc root, beating them into round disks, and cooking them over fires made with sticks and stones.

We were to learn many more things in the ten days we lived among them.

Witnessing In the Nude

Several naked Indians met us at the landing of the plane. They would beat one hand on their chest repeating a phrase. Theirs was a language unknown to the civilized world and was still being recorded by my missionary friends.

Jim and I held our small children tightly in our arms. Since the children were fully clothed, the natives could not tell their genders and they started pulling at their clothes. Sandra quickly told the curious folks the gender of our children. They continued to repeat something and beat their chest. We just smiled as they repeated something to us and crowded around us. They were saying something that sounded like "djeduseabatu".

I turned to Sandra and asked, "What are they saying? Asking?"

She smiled and replied, "They are asking if God lives in your chest."

Oh, glory! A naked Indian had just witnessed to me.

Their language was recorded after years of faithful work by our linguist friend Sandra Cue and others. The Word of God was translated and taught, and now God lived in their chests. And I will see them in heaven one day. (Thankfully they will have on their white robes.)

On the compound the missionaries had cleared out, there were log cabins for the married couples with their children. Bob and Gay Cable, and the Fritz Harter family. There was another cabin for the single ladies. Sandra was the linguist and Maria the nurse. Soon a teacher Edith joined their team and became our friend.

All the houses had an Indian porch on the front where the Indians would come and sit and look into their homes. Not much for privacy, but before they had designed the Indian porches, the Indians felt free to just walk in their hones unannounced.

There was no electricity and indoor plumbing, of course. A generator was saved for certain hours. Jim and three-and-a-half-year-old Kemper went to a nearby shallow stream. They said there was a bench made of bamboo in the middle of the stream so they could sit down while they soaped themselves. They said the water was clear but very cold.

On the last day there they were finally allowed to go to the missionaries' house and take a shower, like little Cindy and I did. The 'shower head" was made from a bucket with holes in the bottom. The water came from above and not from a stream. But it was still cold.

Arrow Stuck in the Shoulder

One day the children and I were in the single missionaries' cabin by ourselves. Jim had gone with missionary Bob and some Indians on an overnight hunting trip with Indians.

My children were taking a nap in the missionary ladies' cabin when I heard a noise at the back steps. Someone calling? I certainly couldn't speak their language if it were a native. Yes, sure enough, there was a young Indian lady sitting on the back step instead of the Indian porch out front. With a long arrow sticking into her naked shoulder!

I looked around to see if the shooter was close by. I knew I needed to run for Maria or Sandra, but I hesitated. The children were still sleeping, and the wounded young lady was still sitting on the back steps. Needing help. I breathed a prayer, "Lord, tell me what to do. " RUN! RUN!

I left the sleeping children and the hurting lady, and ran to the Infirmary building where Maria was. Soon Maria and Sandra were treating the wounded woman as she told them her story in her native tongue. Her husband had shot her with the arrow out of jealousy. He thought that a man from another tribe was trying to steal his woman. (Which she denied.) I was glad she was taken and treated before the children awoke.

Snack in a Banana Leaf

One day we were invited to visit *a maloca* with Sandra. She said it was a huge, round Indian house shaped like a donut. The hole in the thatched roof was to let the smoke escape from the fire in the center to fend off the cold nights. About one hundred Indians lived in a common house with only hammocks hanging all around inside the thatched dwelling. The hammocks were made from homemade spun cotton threads. We watched the women spin from a cotton ball inside a crude hand-held instrument made of twigs.

"Are you folks ready for a hike?" asked Sandra.

'Sure. Let's go since we came to learn all we can."

"It will be an hour's hike straight up," she warned.

"Okay. Let's do it anyway," we agreed. We had no idea what was ahead of us that memorable day.

We left the children with a missionary family that had children. We hiked up the mountain following Sandra and the Indians trying not to lag behind like city folk. We pulled at plants to help us up and sometimes I wished for someone to push me from behind. The canopy over and around us shaded us from the sun, but the humidity made our clothes stick to us. The twigs and thorns scratched me through my skirt and the sweat bees were biting my legs.

Finally, we made it. It was beautiful up there, I'm sure, but all I could see were swarms of naked people coming out of the *maloca* to meet us. They would squeeze Jim's arms and, once they saw his gold-filled teeth, they pulled at his chin for him to open his mouth. They picked up his arm and placed his ticking watch close to their ears. Poor Jim. He just laughed and let them do it.

I hated to say anything, but I whispered to Sandra that I was thirsty after that hike. She turned to one of the Indians and spoke something in his language. She told me that they would go get me some water.

"Is it very far?" I whispered.

"It will be an hour down the mountain and then back up again, " she whispered back.

"Oh, dear. Forget it."

From her smile I think that was exactly the answer she expected.

She told me that the Indians were about to offer us a snack of something that they only harvested one a year.

"What is it?" we whispered.

She said, "Just eat it and smile like a good missionary, remembering that you are the honored guests."

They picked up a big banana leaf from the smoky ashes on the ground and unrolled them carefully. In the center I saw what resembled pecans or peanuts. I had a hunch they were not.

Sandra accepted one and smiled at Jim and me when it came our turn. I prayed silently, Lord, help it go down and stay down. It tasted smoky on my tongue, but I certainly didn't intend to chew it, whatever it was. It went down.

I looked to Sandra for an explanation, but she was talking to the Indians in their language so I waited. Guess what? Sure enough, once a year they harvested this delicacy and had just shared them with us. *Manduruva'*. Larva. Larva? Larva! I really did want a drink of water then.

On the way back down the mountain we followed Sandra and the Indians again. This time I held onto vegetation to keep from sliding down. I noticed the native men and women hiking along with us. The custom is for the Indian women to carry the heavy loads and the men to carry only their bows and arrows.

We followed one young woman with a heavy load of bananas on her head. Probably a stalk of over sixty bananas. Sandra said the woman had been mute for a few years.

Demon possession. After we left the jungle to go on stateside assignment in the USA, I prayed off and on for that young woman. One day Sandra wrote that the young woman accepted Christ, had been delivered of the demon and was talking once again. Praise God.

Linguist Labors

While there in the Amazon my mind was open to the beauty and power of the Scriptures as they shared the challenges of explaining passages that were difficult for the native Indians to visualize.

For example, Jesus spoke of how he would like to gather His people "under His wing like a mother **hen**". Those Indians had never seen a hen. The missionary pilot had to fly in eggs for the families. The pilots also flew in powdered milk since there were no cows in the jungle. The Bible also mentions dogs and horses, but these also were unknown to the uncivilized native people.

The missionary linguists were trying to find the natives vocabulary for the story about Paul's **shipwreck.** There were no rivers or ocean near their jungle compound, and those Indians did not use canoes or boats, much less ships.

John referred to Jesus as the **lamb** who took away the sin of the world. Since they had never seen a lamb, the missionaries had the pilots fly in a lamb and a hen as object lessons for their Bible translations. The next morning, the natives proudly offered the animals to the missionaries – shot with arrows. They couldn't understand how anyone would keep an animal around that wasn't meant for food!

Another interesting story they told was how they made their first primers. In the beginning the linguists had to depend on gestures and signs by listening to the Indians' vocabulary for certain objects. They told how their first primers were full of errors, and some of their stories were hilarious.

One example: They would point to an object and when the Indian made a sound, they would phonetically write it down. They would point to a wooden table and the Indian would say something like: 'xxx". They wrote it down. They pointed to a wooden chair. In Indian said: "xxx". Humm. Well, maybe since the Indians don't have tables and chairs, the missionary linguist pointed to a tree. The Indian would say: "xxx". Perhaps "s=xxx" meant "wood"?

Whenever they came to a puzzling situation, they moved on to something else. Later on, after they had many lists of new vocabulary, they discovered something.

Indians don't use their fingers to point at an object!

They use their noses, not their finger (xxx). So, each time the missionary pointed to an object using his/her finger, the native would say the word for finger (xxx). Sometimes pages would have to be cancelled out because of such errors, but they kept on working.

After years of tedious labor and dedication, portions of the bible were translated and taught to open hearts. The Bible asks "How shall they believe if they have not heard....?" The Indians didn't have a written language. Now they do. They didn't have the Word in their language. Now they do. Now the native believers can preach the Word to others in their own language.

People who walked in darkness, directed by demon spirits now have "Jesus in their chest" and are walking in the light.

The Indians taught us some songs in their native language. They didn't have a wide note range, but I still remember one and hum it often.

Living with the Uai-Uai Indians and the Yanomami Indians those few days, I found that most of their backgrounds included torture from demons. Since demons are the fallen angels who lived in heaven. Saw the glory. Knew Jesus as the Son of God. It was not surprising to read in the Bible that even the demons believed in God. They cried out that Jesus was the Son of God.

I read the testimony of a converted Yanomami shared by a missionary, Gary Dawson. I discovered that the converts testified that the demons could describe to them heaven and it got me to thinking about it even more. The fallen angels/demons had been there. The demons told them about the beauty beyond compare. Nobody was ever hungry, and they never go sick. No death. They even told them that it was in the Heaven of heavens.

However, their leader, Lucifer Satan, has convinced them to tell their victims that the Great Spirit is 'selfish'. That He would not share heaven with them. The Great Spirit was the Enemy God. They feared and hated Him.

But those days before our eyes were men and women who heard the Word of God for the first time. The Truth had peeled away the darkness as the missionaries shared the glorious news of the gospel.

Those naked Indians were concerned to know if I had Jesus in my chest. Makes you think. Glory for the Power in the Word!

Since that experience years ago, I have enjoyed contributing to and promoting the ministries that are translating the Bible in many languages. Our son was born in Brazil and was a business man and a Gideon there.   Go linguist missionary!

Now it was time to pack up, doctor the sweat bee whelps on my body, gather up my sweet children and say good-bye to those wonderful missionary friends.

After five years we were heading back to our "other home" and back to our dear family members.

Chapter Four

First State Side Assignment - 1969

California, Here We Come.

It was near Christmas time and we went to California to see my parents. It was very similar to a Brazilian December. No snow and green vegetation, fruit trees and palm trees all around. We were to introduce my parents to their grandchildren they had never seen. Now that I am a grandparent and have been separated from my grandchildren by continents and years, I can understand their feelings better.

Wow! Surprise. When we arrived at the parsonage, all my sisters and brother and their families were there. What a reunion.

Once again there was so much to catch up on. Our talented, loving Mother had made us girls matching clothes. Our Father told funny stories to entertain us and made sure mother had plenty of food for us to prepare for the big group.

Mother and Father were happy with California and with the church ministry. The people seem to love them. Just a reminder that God takes care of all of us when we follow His plans. "When we are absent one from another."

There were lots of children there to mix with our two little ones. Just one thing, the language barrier. Our children were bi-lingual. They were understanding the English, but would only speak in Portuguese. They were three years old and one-and seven-months years old. But the children adjusted quickly.

People would ask, "What did she say?" "What is he saying?" The two would just smile and wait for us to explain. One thing the folks still remember about our curious little Cindy was that she stuck a metal hair lift into a plug-in. Sparks flew and her tiny figures turned black. We rushed her to the hospital and soon she was on the mend. However, that hindered her thumb sucking for a few days.

But soon the children were playing together and the adults were swapping photos and stories. They had many questions, of course, about our five years away from them. But we could certainly magnify the Lord with each answer.

In downtown Modesto, the four of us were riding in a car sightseeing with my parents. Kemper was curiously playing with the door handle when suddenly he got sucked out of the car. A Volkswagen Van was coming straight at him. I automatically jumped out of the rolling car and pulled him back away from the danger. Our car had stopped when they realized what was happening. A red light soon caught the other traffic and we were safely back into the car. God was looking out for us that year of many months on the road. The children were good travelers and charmed people from coast to coast.

Too soon we needed to leave California, but we had another family waiting to see us.

Next Stop, Florida

Our plane landed in Miami, Florida, and Jim's family was there. Just to see from the windows of the plane the waving American flags my eyes became teary and my chest swelled. I felt safe. I love my country!

Jim's sister, Judy Puckett, married one of Jim's college roommates and they were pastoring the Deerfield church in Florida. Jim and Judy Puckett, met us at the airport and took us to their house in Pompano Beach. They had two little girls, Lancia and Marci.

Jim's other sister, Nancy, and her husband, Ed Cook, pastored in Florida at that time and were also at the airport. Ed was another one of Jim's college roommates. We had a great visit and had much to rejoice over while sharing God's leading and blessings in all of our ministries since Bible College in Nashville, Tennessee. We were all beginning our Summer Season in life.

Our two small children at first had lots of questions. They understood English, but our relatives did not understand their Portuguese. They were born into a bi-lingual family and were confused that these new relatives didn't understand them. They noticed that their little cousins look more like them than their Brazilian playmates.

We didn't have a television in our homes in Brazil and they were impressed with the beautiful wood cabinet of their console T.V. So was I. They commented on several things they were seeing for the first time.

Little Cindy came out of their bathroom informing me.

"Mamae, que bonito. O papel higiencio esta estampado com flores."

Our relatives asked what she was saying. She had said that the toilet paper was pretty and had flowers stamped on it. I had never seen it either.

Blue Bird?

My mother told me on the phone that my niece, Deborah Sue, was going to loan us her little blue Camaro to use in our travels while in the USA.

I said, "How sweet, mother. But I don't know how well we can take care of blue bird while traveling so much."

Mother laughed, "Oh, honey, it is a little blue car. A Camaro." There was a lot to catch up on.

We picked the car up later in Owasso, Oklahoma. It was really something compared to our Brazilian Volks Vans and Jeeps passed down from other missionaries. Her car was a 1968 Rally Sport, teal with a black strip around to the front. It was a three-speed automatic floor console shift. In Brazil we drive standard shift cars. It had black seats and carpet. Deborah's father bought her a 1970 burgundy and white Malibu. Did you notice the O.U. colors? Faithful alumni family.

Next, we were taken to Jim's folks. They and their sons-in-law and daughters were all pastoring in Florida. They seemed so content and it was good to see them after all those years. Their youngest son, Scotty was not much older than our three-year-old Kemper.

One funny thing that happened was at my in-laws' house. They were the parents of 15 children, 14 were living at that time. Jim was their third to the oldest and with him and his sister there they had all their children under one roof. We left to visit a Pastor Dale Burden near their house and left my teen-age brother-in-law Johnny to watch the little boys at home.

When we returned to their home that evening, underneath the Christmas tree was a pile of unwrapped gifts with bows and paper, and boxes scattered. The six little boys were quiet and subdued.

I believe that Mom and Pop Wiley were living in Miami at that time and Benito and Carmen Rodriguez were starting a Cuban church at that time. It was a good place to live and minister at that time.

But where for our family to live during our year of stateside assignment? My father was pastoring in Modesto, California and Jim's father was in Eau Galle, Florida. My sister, Dean, offered a one-bedroom apartment right in front of the Free Will Baptist Church my father had built on Atlanta Street in Owasso, Oklahoma. So that is where we would make our headquarters when we arrived in 1969.

Owasso, Oklahoma

When I arrived at the Tulsa International Airport with my little family, the familiar surroundings seemed to call out, Welcome Home.

My husband had been to Oklahoma, of course, but even though the children were small, I was glad to have them in Owasso with me for the first time.

My niece had her little 1968 Rally Sport Blue Camaro ready for us when we arrived.

We moved into the one-bedroom apartment my sister, Dean, had provided. There were several of her apartments right in front of the Free Will Baptist Church where I was a founding member when in high school. The young Rev. Bob Ketchem was the pastor. His father, Rev. Bill Ketchem, and wife were good friends of our family. How refreshing it was to worship with that wonderful group and receive spiritual nourishment. While not on the road visiting churches, I didn't have to write, translate and produce material to be taught to others to minister .I could receive. I had hot water in the sinks. Heater in the winter and air conditioner in the summer.   We were thankful for so many things.

The apartment was furnished so it was easy just to unpack and get settled. The living room and kitchen were in one small open room. The one bedroom had a bunk bed for the children and then our full-size bed. On the wall in front of the small bathroom hung the telephone. There were no cell phones at that time. It was our lifeline to communicate with all the churches, colleges, and families that would accept our meeting with them to report on what God was doing in the "Sleeping Giant", as Brazil was called by some. The free rent helped us gather our support more quickly. Some Go and some Send. God blessed.

It was the first time that the children had seen snow and they made a fine snowman with Jim's help. It was one of the experiences I wanted them to have that year. It would be at least four more years before they could see it again.

At another one of the apartments, I met Nadine Monroe and her little son Jeff. She became such a sweet friend at a time when I needed one and we attended church together. Kemper and Jeff filled up many hours playing superheroes. One day they decided they would jump off the balcony of one of the apartments like Superman. Jeff jumped and broke both his legs! As you can imagine, Kemper never jumped.

Dean and her family had a lovely home across the street from us. We had several family meetings there and even had Kemper's fifth birthday party there. She had a swimming pool which was another first experience for Cindy and Kemper. Kemper was gifted a bicycle which he could not take with him to Brazil.

Since our children were not school age, we traveled a lot as a family to appointments in churches and district meetings, women's and men's meetings, and youth camps. When we were not traveling, we attended my home church in Owasso.

One day I answered our phone on the wall. It was from Jim. For some reason we had not gone with him to his home state of West Virginia. Probably because he had flown there. Before we hung up, I had promised to pack up the children and drive to West Virginia in our little blue car.

When I discovered we were expecting a baby again I started marking appointments with a Christian doctor friend, Dr. Lloyd Huneryager. (1925-2003). I was so blessed to have a Christian doctor and one that speaks ENGLISH! I remember he was active in the Christian Business Men organization. He quoted scripture to me. At one appointment I had a few minor issues and I mentioned that I didn't have much strength that day. He told me that my "strength comes from the Lord" so I didn't need to depend on my strength. Amen, Sir Doctor.

It was time to return to Brazil and I was in my eighth month. We needed to hurry back to Brazil so the baby would be born there like the other two. The doctor did okay my traveling by plane and we hurried to make it in time! It was a refreshing time with family and friends and wonderful supporters in my own country. But our hearts were turned to our "adopted" field that God had given us. We were homesick to get back to our beloved Brazil. First stop would be in Campinas, SP, to have our baby girl.

Chapter Five

Second Term in Brazil-1971

The Field Council missionaries all contributed to have a mission apartment in the city of Campinas, Sao Paulo, where the first *Igreja Batista Livre* church began. It was a large city with good doctors, hospitals and business and was our official mission headquarters address. All of us had keys and could use it anytime we needed to.

The mission apartment was our first stop after landing at the International Airport. It was a long all-night flight but we all made it okay. While we waited for our baby to be born in a few days, I checked in with a Christian doctor there in Campinas. We didn't have technology to tell us the gender of the baby, but Kemper and Cindy gave suggestions on what to name the baby.

Since I had caesarian sections with our other children, I had a talk with the doctor. I told him that we had wanted at least four children and that I would like to try to have a natural birth this time. Try to see if there would be dilation this time before trying another caesarian procedure. He said NO!

I mentioned that the Kennedy women in the USA had more than three caesarian births. He explained that if I were rich enough to stay in bed for nine months and have someone else care for me and my family, he still wouldn't agree. He said that it was not the outer scar that would be the problem. It was the scar on the uterus that could burst with another caesarian. So, that idea was settled. One more caesarian coming up soon.

While waiting, a professional photographer passed among the apartments offering his services. He took great photos of our two children while we were waiting for the next one. We enjoyed the photos so much and then they were swept away years later in a mass flood of our city. Two years after that they appeared at our door in the hands of a stranger. Amazing little gifts from Father God.

Missionaries John and Connie Craft were living in Campinas at the time in language school. Kemper and Cindy enjoyed getting acquainted with them and their three girls those days. We visited with them one night and I had to climb a few steps to the house. By the time I reached their door, my back and leg pain were quite strong and Connie, a nurse, had me lie down. My pain continued. My time was getting near.

Baby Number Three, Tania

My overnight bag was packed and ready to go to the hospital any moment. We had one run to the hospital, but they said it was false labor pain, so we returned to the apartment.

The next day we knew it was the real thing so we took Kemper and Cindy to the Crafts' house and Jim took me to the hospital. On May 26th, 1971 beautiful little Tania Marita was born. "Marita' means little Mary or Marie after my mother. Jim had met a lady at a golf course in the States by that name and suggested we use it if the baby were a girl. Tania was a name we thought would be easy to pronounce in both languages.

Two days later Cindy had her third birthday and the children were still at the Craft's house. Since baby Tania and I were still in the Campinas hospital, Aunt Connie made a blue bunny rabbit birthday cake for Cindy. Connie and I were bonded in God's love and calling during those days that she served our family.

Before traveling south to our next assignment, we dedicated our new baby at the Campinas FWB Church. Missionary 'Uncle" Earnie Deeds officiated.

Team Focus on the South

Our mission was a member of MIB (Missionary Information Bureau) at that time. We had written to them to ask information about the neediest area in Brazil at that time for the Gospel of Jesus Christ. Their answer was – Santa Catarina. Two states below our state of Sao Paulo. We had the blessing of the Brazil Field Council of Free Will Baptist missionaries to pursue that possibility.

We wrote to cities in that state stating that we would like to move to their area and be a blessing to their citizens. We waited. Prayed. Waited. The only city in the state of Santa Catarina that answered us was the city of Tubarao (Shark City).

Sam and June Wilkinson with their children –Kevin, Kimberly, and Kenan, and John and Connie Craft and their three girls, had met with us to plan the planting of a church in a needy community. Making contacts was important for friendship evangelism. We discussed plans and laid them before the Lord to eliminate or to bless.

One plan was to invite neighbors and other contacts into our homes for special holiday celebrations, family birthdays, and other events. Our children would help us with making contacts for that. Our visitors would observe our attitudes and customs. There were no more Americans in town and very few Protestant Christians. Some contacts would come from curiosity at least.

Another plan was to open a Reading Room downtown with Christian books in Portuguese addressing pertinent topics of the day. Bibles and magazines in Portuguese. Christian music enhancing reading, and tables for chess and checkers, and a ping-pong table. We would offer English conversations around the tables for those who were interested. All to attract and evangelize.

After making the contacts, we would invite folks into our home to see Moody Science films. They were quality, colorful films showing amazing scientific facts and giving a gospel application at the conclusion.

While reaching city neighborhoods where we would live, we were considering going to the grist mills surrounding the city and offering prayer and assistance. Corn was ground with the help of a water wheel near a water source to make corn meal and other products. Several people were employed there.

Each missionary family considered his or her spiritual gifts and strengths and where they could fit in the plans for planting a church in that city for the glory to God.

Jim and John Craft went on the long trip to the city of Tubarao to look at the housing situation for three families. It was about 18 hours on a sleeper bus, and a little less by car. The practice at that time, and until now, was to rent only if you had a co-signer to be responsible for the obligation. Well, no one knew them in town to be co-signer, but it seems God led them to the right people because that requirement was waived in each case.

Another preparation they made for our houses was transformers. All of our electrical appliances we were moving there were 110 watts. The whole city of Tubarao was 220 watts. Jim and John ordered and placed transformers in the houses. By the time Sam and June's family arrived, I believe their house already had a transformer ordered.

Shark City Receives the Gringos

When baby Tania was one month old, the two missionary families moved two states to the south of us in June, 1971. . Tubarao, Santa Catarina. It was a very rainy day. The Sam Wilkinson family arrived a few months later in August, after they returned from State-side Assignment. Later a young Brazilian evangelist, Ivan Lopes, joined us.

How wonderful to have a team to face the opportunities to share the gospel with a needy people. Our first meetings were just our three families and Ivan. Then the Lord started sending more.

When we went to the neighbor's homes, we asked to talk to the man of the house. We taught that the man is the spiritual leader of the family so we targeted the male population. In all our experiences we knew that women were sensitive to spiritual needs for themselves and for their families. Since I was a daughter of a preacher and a granddaughter of a preacher, I had seen how important the female element was in any church plant.

Some were reached by contact with our children and visiting in our home on special occasions. We home schooled our children in English and then those old enough went to public schools. They helped to make contacts. Also, their dentists and pediatricians were fascinated with our little blond, blue-eyed children who could speak both languages. Contacts. Connie Craft was expecting a baby while there, so there was more bonding as she went through that in a foreign land. Contacts.

Some were reached at the Reading Room and English conversations. Sam Wilkinson and son, Kevin, went there daily. There was an Open House event with a special reception of American food. One of the first contacts was Gabriel Cassao. A teenager who responded and found the faith he was seeking. He learned English from our children and became an English teacher. He married a Christian woman.

Some were neighbors who came to our home for the Moody Science Films. The Lavino Thiizon families of brothers and sisters were our neighbors and came into our home to watch the films. They continued to participate for the following years. The Aguiars were next door neighbors. The parents were teachers and they allowed three of their children to actively participate in our services. Milton, Jr. Jaqueline, and Leticia.

The Mendes family were neighbors to the Crafts and many of them attended our activities. The mother, a daughter, and sons attended. One son, Jose' Pedro, accepted Christ as Savior and became a missionary pilot. He was a passenger on a plane in the Amazon going to his base and died when the plane crashed. His family members that were baptized and faithful to attend, were so proud that one of their sons was in ministry. After his death, they were visited by the Jehovah's Witnesses. We had moved from there and when we returned on a visit, they turned over to us his Bible and Christian text books from his Bible studies. They had been convinced that he was following a false cult and now was not in heaven. My heart was pierced. Sad. We must follow up in situations like this to warn hurting lambs against wolves in sheep clothing.

A couple started attending and the husband offered to play the pump organ in the living room. He had studied to become a priest and then searched the Scriptures to answer his questions. He taught our young Kemper how to play the organ, but his little short legs would hardly reach the pump pedal.

A local priest visited a few times and commented that he agreed with our teachings, but he couldn't afford to break with his faith since he was a professor in a parochial school. He spoke good English and enjoyed conversing with the Gringos.

One day John Craft invited a priest to go ocean fishing with them. A huge storm brought giant waves beating on their boat and the priest was very fearful. He wrapped himself and prayed Hail Mary's as the storm increased. John stood up and sang in Portuguese, *"Com Cristo no Barco Tudo Vai Muito Bem"* (With Christ in the boat you can smile at the storm!) They were all glad to be back on dry land. Contacts.

While contacting new people, one group was impressed by John and Sam. There was a tobacco company in town, Reynolds Company. John checked on their smoke stack to see which way the wind was blowing before going fishing. When

Sam and John visited with the men working there, the workers were surprised that those Gringos knew about tobacco growing. Sam was from Georgia and John from North Carolina. They had grown up around tobacco farms. The workers were surprised that those states used some of the same processes that they used in the Brazil. More contacts were important.

Each family added to the team effort in special ways. We covered more areas and made more contacts with our team of six adults and nine children. But the lifelong bonding as "family" lasts beyond one generation.

One thing the men did together. There was no place in our state to exchange our mission salary into Brazilian currency. The men went once a month to the city of *Porto Alegre,* south in the state *of Rio Grande de Sul.* It took several hours to make the trip and they had to arrive at the bank to make the exchange before 11:00 am. Why? The bank and other businesses closed down for the *siesta* from 11:00 am to 1:00 pm.

After one o'clock, the men could go shopping for food items we couldn't find in our state. Among other things, they looked for cereal. There were only two kinds of cereal at that time - Corn Flakes and Rice Krispies, and they were expensive. But it was one of the things the families looked forward to when they arrived. Once Sam brought back a little dog named, "Lolita", a feisty little thing. Our kids inherited it when they left the area. That was an adventure.

Growing in Numbers

Our living room had many long windows on two walls which I covered with shear curtains. Sofas, kitchen chairs, lawn chairs and our pump organ bench held neighbors and friends as they watched the Moody Science Films.

We had a carport in front of our house. Sometime in the past a garage had been closed in for a bonus room in the house. We used that for Sunday School room for children and youth. Jim built a portable puppet stage and he and I taught Bible stories and songs from the puppets "Gilberto e Susie".

The small group started growing in numbers so we needed a larger place. Five had been baptized in the local river and were in discipleship classes. Others went to Catholic mass first and said they could hardly wait to get to our services on time.

Okie Family Visitors

When relatives came to visit us, our children were able to show their beloved Brazil to relatives on those rare visits. In the forty-four years my parents, Jim's parents, one of Jim's sisters, one of my sisters and family visited us. Our children were able to show their Brazil to relatives. We missed our family and wanted to share our beloved Brazilian people and culture with them.

In 1973 my sister, Dean, and her family, Herbert, Debbie, Eddie, Danny, and my mother Marie landed in the Sao Paulo airport. There they took another plan to travel south to the Florianopolis, Santa Catarina airport to visit us. The second flight faced turbulence so some were not feeling well to make their road trip to reach our house in Tubarao.

But, oh, how wonderful it was to see our own family. There were greetings, hugs, and lively conversation. We loved to see the reaction of our Brazilian friends to our friendly family from

Oklahoma. They wanted to know if they saw many cowboys and Indians, an impression they got from American movies.

After visiting in our city of about 50 years behind the USA, they went to the great beach city, the modern and famous Rio de Janeiro. They visited the *Cristo Redentor* statue overlooking the city and beautiful beaches. It is listed as one of the New7Wonders of the World. It is a statue of Jesus Christ with His arms stretched out, created by a French sculptor. It is 30 meters tall, on an eight-meter pedestal, and its arms stretch 28 meters wide. The place is beautiful. It draws huge crowds. We went before the age of "selfie" cameras, but we took photos which included other tourists in the background.

Next was a visit to Sugar Loaf Mountain. We could see it from the statue of Christ. There was a long line to buy tickets. We reached the top by cable car at an elevation of 1,296 feet. That in itself was a scenic ride. Once there we saw a spectacular view of the city and beaches. Walking around we saw souvenir shops, snack shops and tourists of many nationalities watching the little monkeys hop around freely among the trees and benches. Of course, more photos. All the time we were translating and interpreting for our families.

Vai Com Deus, Queridos

The John Cowart family was near the end of their term and they left for their state-side- assignment. The Wilkinson's were assigned by the Field Council to move back to Jaboticabal, SP, for an urgent need there at Evangelandia camp ground and the church. We would miss them so much. (Especially the wonderful fish stew and biscuits that Connie Craft made us, after the guys came back from deep sea fishing.) But they each had helped us plant a new church family with their variety of talents and gifts and helped train Brazilians to help us carry on the plan God had for the city.

Strange Advertisement

When we reach out to the community to serve, the citizens notice. When we represent the compassionate Lord Jesus and give even a cup of cold water in His name, it feels right and good. Jesus himself said that when we see someone hungry, thirsty, or a foreigner in our midst and we fulfill their need, we are doing it unto Him. We tried to help the poor and teach English in schools that begged for our help. One opportunity appeared at our gate. And reappeared. Many times.

If anyone has been to Brazil, there is a great chance that he or she has been approached by beggars. We saw many during our time in Brazil and I will tell you about one as an example of how complicated it can be.

One of the beggars became a regular customer at our house. Those in the neighborhood were not too comfortable with it.

Anthony was the town mascot. A handsome young man probably in his twenties. He had no family and was mentally challenged, but showed no outward sign. As he went from merchant to merchant downtown, they were patient and friendly. Unfortunately, the cheapest drink they offered him was white lightning from sugar cane. So, the town mascot became the town drunk. The town gave him the nickname "Toninho Louco." (Crazy Little Tony.)

At times he would stop Jim on the downtown streets and start a string of disconnected terms in English he had picked up from different places. His pronunciation was not bad.

"Hey, what time is it? United State of America, my friend. President Richard Nixon, Hello, my friend, how are you? What time is it? United states of America..."

Brazilians passing by would stop and listen. They knew he had limitations. Since English was a required language studied in public school and colleges, most found it difficult to learn.

Jim always got a chuckle out of it because Toninho really was speaking English, but they didn't ask if it made any sense.

When he clapped at our gate, however, he was speaking in Portuguese. Sometimes we would have him take a bath in a shower in our little laundry area on the back porch. We would pour medicine on the open sores on his legs after the bath. He yelled and complained. One sore was so fierce looking that Jim wanted to take him to the hospital but he really became upset and refused to go. We told them about our Lord and we wanted to show him the Lord's love, also.

In Portugues he pleaded, "If my wounds heal, people on the street would not have pity on me and will not help me." He thought he had to pick off the scabs so that they would keep oozing!

Sometimes Toninho would come to our gate asking for a place to sleep. At first, we would put him on a pallet on the floor of the screened in back porch. Oh, no! He would urinate and the smell was terrible. We had to throw away the pallet blankets.

He didn't come very often, but no one wanted to face the clean up again.

Jim found a hammock made of nylon mesh which he hung on the screened-in front porch for the children. The next time Toninho came asking to sleep, we let him sleep in the hammock on the front porch. Early the next morning Toninho was gone and there was a puddle on the tile floor under the hammock. We could open up the water hose to wash the floor of the porch and the hammock quickly dried after being washed in hot soapy water. We thought we had it worked out, but he took us by surprise on another visit.

One night somehow, we forgot to lock our Volks Variant station wagon. A rare thing. There was no sign of Toninho that night, but as soon as we opened the car door, we knew without a doubt that he had been there. The smell was overwhelming, and after all the cleaning and disinfectant, it lingered for days. The children really didn't want to get in the car, and who could blame them?

Once Toninho arrived with scratches on his face and arms. He said he had fallen because of a seizure. Jim cleaned him up and doctored his wounds. Jim gave him one of his nice shirts, pants, socks, and shoes. He really looked proud and waved from the gate as he went to the corner and turned.

Later Jim came into the house really upset. One of the neighbors told him that as soon as Toninho got out of sight, he sold the clothes and shoes for a few pennies. Jim said he was going to be ready for Toninho when he returned.

One day the young man arrived at the gate, and gave his same greetings with a smile.

Jim said, "Toninho, if you ever need something to eat or a place to sleep, we will help you out. But I will never, never give you clothes and shoes again. You deceive me and accept my good clothes and turn around and sell them for pennies."

Toninho was shocked and had an answer to that.

Translated into English Toninho said, "Why you low down, dirty dog, you. After all I have done for you."

Jim asked, "Toninho, what in the world have you ever done for me?"

"Why, I have told all over town what a nice man you are. I have invited lots of people to come here to your house for Bible studies," he replied.

After he left, Jim commented. "No wonder our congregation is so slow in growing, with that kind of advertising."

Evidently, Toninho got over it because he would return off and on, but never again did Jim waste his good clothes on him.

We can say that it is not easy. Just remember that Jesus paid a high price to help his fellowman and to show compassion while he was on this earth and an even higher price on the cross to offer salvation to all of us.

What an honor when He has asked us to do the same thing as His ambassador on this planet. If we try it, it feels right and good.

Hosting Foreigners at Our Gate

After the other missionaries left, we were the only Americans in town which gave us a unique opportunity to entertain foreigners. We home schooled our children so it was an opportunity for them, too.

The last coal fed steam locomotive in the country of Brazil is in our city of *Tubarao* which was a tourist attraction to those from other countries. Some of our new Christians worked for the train agency. Jim's home state, West Virginia, was a coal mining area, too. Officials asked us to host them and they ended up sitting at our table for a meal. They usually didn't speak Portuguese and their English wasn't easy to understand. But we were able to communicate and gain a wealth of experiences.

There was a Frenchman and we thanked him for the statue of Liberty. An Englishmen appeared at out gate for a Brazilian meal and we thanked him for our motherland. A Jewish man was sitting at our table, and I thanked his people for Jesus, our Jewish Messiah. He only nodded his head.

Some compatriots also visited us. One example was Robert and Deanna Grider, and sons, Clifton and Craig. Not only were they Americans but they were from Oklahoma and Free will Baptist. They were working in an American School for businessmen and military families in the beautiful city of Curitiba, Parana.

A man from Germany and his wife from Japan were traveling around the world by bike. I saw their sign on their bike and introduced myself. They were glad to hear someone speak English. They didn't speak Portuguese and I certainly didn't speak German or Japanese. I invited them to our house for a meal and for the family to meet them.

They shared with our family that they recorded their journeys, and the National Geographic Magazine was interested in their adventures and photos.

The children loved to hear their stories and adventures. Countries, continents, mountains, deserts, beaches, and forests. They packed a tent, cooking equipment, food and first aid, and hygiene products strapped to their bikes. They were impressed at how often they had to buy bike tires and how they had to eat delicious candy bars every four hours to give them energy for hours and hours of riding their bikes.

They stayed for a couple of days and enjoyed hot baths and getting caught up on equipment repair and food supply. We wanted to give them something for their trip, but they only suggested the Brazilian equivalent of packages of Kool-Aid. It was a small gift in exchange for the rich and fascinating experience given to our family.

They accepted a prayer before they biked away from our gate. Hospitality is good.

Little Missionary Children

Our children were helpful in making our home the happy place it was. We had no idea what God had for each of them but for the oldest, his spiritual journey began in Tubarao. Cindy's was on our first state-side assignment, and Tania's was after our return to Tubarao.

Our five-year-old, Kemper, came to me in his pajamas early one morning and said, *"Mamae, quero Jesus no coracao"*.

"You want Jesus in your heart? How wonderful, son!"

We went over the plan of salvation together and prayed. When he raised his head, there were tears in his eyes and my eyes. Our son was praying the same prayer I had used with children since I started teaching Sunday school in the seventh grade.

He ran to his father and said we needed to call his grandparents in Oklahoma and his grandparents in West Virginia to tell them that he got saved and that he was happy.

We had a missionary intern staying at our house and Kemper kept asking him, *"Francisco, esta' feliz?"*

"Yes, Kemper, I am happy," he answered.

Later, "Franciso, ar you happy?"

Yes, Kemper, I am.

Later, "Francisco, are you happy?"

*"Sim, K*emper, but don't you think that you need to sleep now?"

"Okay. *Boa noite."*

"Boa noite. Kemper"

"I'll be happy tomorrow, too."

A mother likes to brag on her children. His "tomorrows" included growing up in Brazil, attending Hillsdale free Will Baptist College, *Seminario Batista Livre,* and *the* University of Central Oklahoma with a degree in Decision Sciences.

In Brazil he owned a Language School in Araras. He served in the church as a Sunday School teacher, a youth sponsor, Assistant Pastor, through an instrumental and vocal ministry.

He also served on the board of *the Lar Nova Vida* Children's Home.

Add three more. A Master's Degree in Education/Teaching Methods, from Araras, SP, Brazil where he was a professor. He taught French and Spanish at Harrah High School. A Master in Business from DeVry/Keller University in Oklahoma City. A Masters in Human Services from Regents University in Virginia. He is presently employed at FARMERS Insurance as part of the Bi-lingual team. He is active in his church men's group and participates in the praise team.

Dead Dog Mystery

One of my new friends was having classes for preparing for baptism. She was the Crafts' neighbor and had offered to help me around the house during a very busy time. After a few days I was sick in bed, so it seemed like a good idea to have the help. I started paying her.

Jim entered my room quietly and sat on the side of the bed. "I came to check on you. I have been talking to the Crafts.

What do you think about spirit possession and Christians?"

It seemed like a strange question at the moment. "I feel that if you are filled with the Holy Spirit, the evil spirits will not be able to enter."

"Well, I have fired your helper. Connie told me some things about her."

I asked, "What things?"

"Connie said that her daughter went to her house and told her that she had found two marked jars. One was marked with her mother's name and it had honey in it. The other jar had some black substance. The daughter opened it and threw it out to the dog and it died. It was marked 'Shirley'."

Witch craft!

"Connie thought that since you are sick, her mother may be putting something in your food. So, I fired her."

She was my friend and I was hurt. But the scriptures teach that the battle is not "against flesh and blood, but against principalities, against power, against the rulers of the darkness of this age". Satan had blinded her eyes. I wanted a chance to tell her that. I saw her a few times after that.

Tragedy Hits Shark City - 1974

Each address has special memories of victories and struggles with God always present. One particular struggle destroyed our house, our car, and our Brazilian city of Tubarao, but not our spirits.

One Saturday in March the river was getting fuller all day. It was about a block from our house. We put our little family in our car and drove through the neighborhoods built along the river side, like ours. A few lower areas had water rising near the houses.

We had seen it full many times but people started to comment "never this high before." Our neighbors, the Aguiars, went with their family to Dehon College a block away. Our neighbor on the other side in his 70's said he lived there all his life and it never flooded on our street. He was not leaving.

We listened to the radio. A lot of rain still falling in the mountains and would be flowing into our already full river.

We put our children to bed in their clothes as a precaution. Jim and Jose Pedro took blankets and sheep skin rugs to the Dehon College in case we needed to take the children there.

Big cables on a footbridge stretching across the river connecting the two sides of the city were torn loose by the raging water and the bridge was swept away.

Jim and Jose Pedro had put up high the washing machine, freezer, and refrigerator. They put drawers on top of the wardrobes. It was hard to believe the water would fill up that high.

After midnight water began running in our garage and on our back porch. The streets were full of people. The main auto bridge on Lauro Muller Street was wiped out.

Our kitchen was filling with water!

Fleeing Through Raging Waters

"Wake up the kids!" Jim exclaimed. "We'd better get over to the school before it gets too bad in the streets."

It was 4:00 am on Sunday morning. It was still raining. Jim carried Kemper, Jose Pedro carried Cindy, and I, Tania. I grabbed my purse and put it high on my shoulder. Water was waist deep.

My shoes were swept off my feet but the water was too swift to try to save them and hold on to my baby, too. The gravel on the street felt like broken glass to my feet. The mud was slippery and we couldn't go fast or we would lose our balance and drop everything. (I went without shoes for the next several days.)

I kept thinking – I need to keep up with the men in front of me. Walking was difficult. I had to protect the child in my arms from the rain and cold wind. I had to force my legs to cut through rolling water. Keep my balance. Don't fall. I had to call out to God to help me not fall.

We found room in classrooms on the second floor of the college where we had given classes. We heard there were two other families there but we didn't see them anywhere. The men had scooted the student chairs together and put the sheep skin rugs and blankets on them to put the children on. They couldn't sleep. They were full of questions. Little Tania started singing a Brazilian folk song. "*Ai, ai, ai, que amor de arvore*". (What a Lovely Tree)

I knew it was a day at a time situation and I found some paper in the class room waste basket. My pen and Portuguese New Testament were in my purse so I kept a diary before the electricity went off.

Food, Water? How?

Jim and Jose Pedro returned quickly to our house that was filling up with water. They put up more things higher on top of tables and counters. They returned with food from our refrigerator that I had made for lunch that day after Sunday School services. We fed the Aguiar's family, our family, and some children.

They tore down my curtains to take to help wrap the folks without blankets. I would never need them again.

By this time there were 80 people in the building so we had to ration out the food starting with the children. Around noon the military sent bread, milk, bananas by fire trucks. With 80 hungry people, it was welcomed but quickly gone. Later a helicopter dropped medicine, dry macaroni and wieners.

We wondered about the people from our new formed Bible Study group? Our college students? Were they safe? Hungry?

That Sunday afternoon we had Bible Club with the children to keep them calm. Parents stood in the door way. I told them stores about Jesus stilling the storm, Noah's Ark and the rainbow of promise. We sang about the animals going safely into the Ark. We sang 'With Christ in the boat we can smile at the storm." I felt it was good for the exhausted, bewildered parents who were listening. My own little children were so good to help.

The radio announced that the military prohibited any more news reports about the rain condition. (We lived under Socialism and Communism so we were accustomed to censorship.) We thought this was a bad sign. The rain did slack up so Jim and Jose returned to the house. They found the water had drained out of the kitchen some. They had jacked up the car and the water hadn't reached the motor. They tried to move it to higher ground, but it would not start.

There was no electricity. The radio was gone.

Was the water deceiving us?

Flooded clock – Monday 1:30 am

Jim decided to rest a while and set the alarm clock to go off at midnight and put the clock on the floor by the bed. Jose Pedro slept on the sofa in the living room.

Jim woke up at 1:00. The water was up to his knees in the bedroom. The clock had been covered by water.

He yelled at Jose Pedro in the living to get out fast. They worked hard to open the door against the force of water. Once they got outside, the swift water carried them away. The current was so swift that they had no control of the direction they were going. The current carried them down the street and threw them into the Dehon School stone wall. Holding onto the top of the wall, part of it broke and threw them to where the soccer field was located in the back of the school.

It was pitch black. The water was roaring. Large objects were swirling past them. Jim yelled at Jose to swim under water to try to reach the building. They reached the building and found a window open. Jose stood on Jim's shoulders and entered. He helped to pull Jim in.

They wrapped themselves in blankets they found. . As they made their way up the stairway, they saw that it was filling up with water.

Jim said to wake up the men. To warn them to go to the floor below and get food, school documents, library books, etc., to a safe place. They started immediately.

Someone found soccer uniforms for Jim and Jose. It gave a comic relief with people teasing them as they walked around the next days in their uniforms.

Jim had big bruises on his legs where he hit the wall. Thank God they were alive! He reported that the water was over the car and at window level in the house. Rain and hard wind again. Water was rising. We decided to have everyone move up to the next floor.

People came out of their rooms with candles they had found. No electricity. They expressed fear. Anguish. They had lost all their material goods.

One man found a bottle of whisky and invited the adults to the conference room to get strength and discuss conditions.

We told them our strength comes from the Lord. We went back to our class room and huddled with our little family.

Monday Sunrise

Sunrise and we were all glued to the windows. Cloudy, rainy, but light enough to see. We tried to believe the roaring waters against our building and covering houses. The whole town was covered. Hospital, banks, schools, businesses. All covered. A town of 70,000 people.

We could see people on rooftops in hard rain signaling for a helicopter. Trapped. Some possibly dead? Human chains of people trying to cross over turbulent water together.

Children squealed as they saw people "swimming". A chill went through our group as we realized that they were dead bodies being carried away. We also saw dogs, cows, horses, and pigs floating by. Some chickens were in the top of tress along with humans.

Semi-trucks were bouncing in the water like toys. The cold wind brought the rain on us but we remained at the windows.

Jim said the ocean, about 15 miles away, must be rejecting the water trying to flow into it. We later found it to be true. Patience and prayer.

Look at the Facts

The group had increased to 85 people in the building. Strangers put together by fate. We had dry rice and macaroni. But no stove. No water. Pan? Plates? Spoons?

We found a Bunsen burner from the science laboratory hooked to a small propane tank. A tiny flame. Someone found a pan. Since all the underground pipes and cables were torn from the earth, folks would be able to cook using their propane tanks. If their stoves and tanks had not floated away.

What about water? Jim found a flexible, black doormat. He held the mat out the window while rain beat against it. He rubbed it with his hands. With the curved mat he made a drain to catch precious water into the pan.

First the precious water was rationed to give to the children. No one could wash their hands. No one seemed to care.

It took hours to cook the rice over the small burner. Seasoning? No salt, oil, onions, garlic. We had a few wieners left. We chopped them and put them in the rice.

The military had left two dozen paper plates. Spoons? We found little aluminum coasters and tore them in half, curved them to make little scoops.

For 85 people we used the paper plates over and over again. The middles were getting a little thin.

When it was time for the next meal, we only had the dry macaroni left. There was no water to wash the rice pan. Hard rice was stuck in the bottom of the pan. Well, we caught more rain water and it took hours for it boil from the tiny Bunsen burner. We plopped the macaroni in water. Once again, no salt. Nothing. Once again, we fed the group one by one. The plates were getting even thinner!

Jim led in prayer from the very first meal but hearts were gradually getting more sincere and more grateful as the days passed by and supplies dwindled.

Vaccinations

The science teacher of the college, Professor Piva, prepared the vaccines from the supplies the helicopter dropped. After floods come epidemics, disease, and snakes. He used the same needles over and over without sterilization!

It was voluntary, but long lines of young and old formed. We stood in a dark, damp, candle-lit room to receive the vaccines. Hepatitis was a concern. At least it was something we could do in the midst of all the chaos.

Questions

The children were getting restless. They didn't want to go near the school rest rooms. The water was rising and the plumbing was backed up in all the systems. The odor was appalling and the sight was atrocious.

We continued with the Bible stories and songs. More and more parents were standing in the doorway. Rain continued to pour and the people were losing patience.

They asked in Portuguese,

"Why isn't God answering prayer? Are we all going to die?" Is it the end of the world?" They began wailing and fainting.

I said, "Our city is destroyed but the whole world is not destroyed. God will send a rainbow of promise, but maybe God is waiting for you to give up your despair and really demonstrate your faith to your family. To your children. Then He will work the miracle. You must believe."

"The Bible says that God set His rainbow in the cloud and made a covenant between Him and every living creature of all flesh, that waters will never again become a flood to destroy all flesh. "(Genesis 9:13-17)

They just stared at me and left.

The Miracle Was Beginning

Praise God! The miracle began. The wind changed in our favor. Encouragement spread. The water level began to lower a few centimeters at a time.

Just before going to bed, the people asked Jim to call everyone together again. They said he was the closest to a priest that they had.

We took our candle stubs to the school chapel.

Jim read from the little Portuguese New Testament I had in my purse, "What shall it profit a man if he shall gain the whole world and lose and own soul?"

He said he knew that all they had gained in this was probably lost out there in the darkness. When tomorrow came they needed to be prepared for it. To know , to really know the personal God of the Bible is worth more than the entire world. Wow!

They were seeing God working. They were more thoughtful. Their attitudes were changed from rebellious to hopeful toward getting out alive and starting over again.

Tuesday Morning- March 26

Everyone was relieved to see the water down sufficiently to wade, but we were shocked to see roads caved in and worn away. The darkness had temporarily protected us from the disastrous scenes outside the window. After going through mud, broken asphalt and water, many found their homes wrecked. Others found no home at all. Much of the town was missing, too.

The hospital, the downtown business section, bridges, schools were all destroyed. No electricity, no water, no means of communication to the outside world. No passable streets.

Our home? From our high window we could see our home. The wall of the front bedroom had collapsed. Most furniture was forced out and washed away. Our pump organ from the living room was face down in the mud and caught in front of the bedroom door.

Many things inside the house were all mixed up and fallen in the mud. We carried back to the school building a few wet, muddy clothes. Clothes on the line on the back porch were not muddy.

The photos and home movies of our three babies' first steps were in the mud. Coin collections, stamp collections, boxes of studies, research, and preparations all lost. All gone. Numb. Somehow those material things didn't seem to matter right then.

We did find that our file cabinet was filled with mud and water and was wedged between a door frame. It was not carried away. In the top drawer was some Brazilian money, the children's birth certificates, our wedding certificate, and other documents that we would be needing. We thankfully laid them out to dry on the desks when we returned to the school.

We were sorry for all the destruction, but were glad that our loss was as heavy as the rest of the neighbors. People would believe us when we encouraged them to trust God to help them start life over again.

Out of Water – More People

We had wanted the rain to stop but now we were out of drinking water. We prayed and prepared buckets to catch it in. God sent rain for 30 minutes and we were prepared. We needed a lot for so many people and to cook rice or macaroni. God provided.

That night the candles were just about gone so the families sang and praised God together in the dark. We prayed for an opening to get information out that we were alive. Jim walked across a broken bridge to the post office to send a telegram. No electricity. No working post office.

More people arrived in our building. 120 people now. They had been in attics and on roof tops. Many came searching for family members. So sad.

Food for 120?

Our house was close by so Jim went back to see what food he could take to the group. Mud was packed on both sides of the doors of the freezer and it was difficult to open. The water had ruined the motor but the food was still frozen. Frozen milk. Frozen rabbits.

Senhor Milton walked to the military station to see about food. They said if you have one meal a day it is more than some. They gave one banana, one sack of water, and one piece of old bread per person. But you had to take your own sack. No sacks! We found a pillow case for us.

Jim and Jose Pedro went to Professor Pedro's house to carry a small stove to the school. Jim tripped and fell and his hand went through the glass door of a hutch nearby. They invented a bandage but there was no water, no hygiene. Just thankful the cut wasn't worse.

Now we had a way to cook. We fried rabbits. They found, among the mud, some bottles of pop in the school snack shop and they handed out one to every three people.

I found some more paper for my notes.

Wednesday – 7:00 am

I heard a strange male voice in the hallway early in the morning. A man came from the state of Parana' and explained that he was looking for his sister and family.

"Is her name Eugenia?" I asked.

"Yes."

"She is my neighbor. Yes, she is right here on this floor. I'll take you to her. She will be so glad to see you."

As we walked thought the hall full of little rain puddles, he told how he had heard the news of the devastating flood on the television and had been on the road in his pickup truck trying to reach Tubarao. I left him alone with his family and went back to mine to talk to Jim. I had an idea.

After they visited for a while, I went back to their room. They were preparing to leave, and she was tying a bundle of clothing in a sheet.

"*Senhor,* excuse me but I would like to ask a favor for my three children and me," I started. Could you give us a ride in the back of your pickup to another city where we can catch public transportation?"

He, his sister and her husband, Milton, looked at each other.

"In the back of the truck will be in the rain, but you are welcome to go with us. You will have to hurry and leave right now. My truck is parked on the edge of town, and we must leave before the bridge is completely washed out. It could go anytime now."

We gathered up the children and the few things we had put in a muddy suitcase Jim had tried to wash out. The money we found in the file cabinet helped us buy tickets and the birth certificates were necessary sine the law requires them when traveling with your children. We had been wearing the same clothes for five days, no baths, and I was still barefooted.

Jim had decided he would stay and check on the others in our church group. Besides, there was not much room for him in the truck!

We walked across town in the rain to the truck and how it hurt my bare feet! While we were thankful that God provided us a way to get in contact with someone, I hated to leave my husband and the others in their hour-by-hour struggles. He, Jose Pedro, Gabriel and Senhor Milton made a pitiful sight as they stood waving to us among the debris that was once a picture postcard city. He was still in the blue and gold soccer uniform with mud to his knees.

On the Road, In the Rain

We were stopped several times on the way. Once, authorities were checking to see if we were "smuggling" out food. Another time, the pick-up crawled across a broken bridge while we walked behind. The third time was because of a caved in pavement – declared impassable. We passed over it.

The next twelve hours involved a truck ride, a plane ride, a bus ride, a taxi ride, and a car ride with strangers. The truck took us to the state north of us. The first leg of our unforgettable journey meant trying to protect my children from the wind and the rain as it fell on us in the back of the truck. It was unbelievable. They didn't complain! We huddled together, and they sat on the old suitcase to cushion the shock of the bounce.

Several times we had to descend from the truck to walk across broken and narrow strips of highway that were left from landslides. We held our breath as the pickup crept across obstacles. The children were so brave. They had not shown fear of the water, the dark nights or the complaints of others.

The power plant in our city served a great region. Its failure strangled the source of electricity for a long way as we stopped for service in the gas stations. At one of these stations, we had our first drink of clear mineral water.

One restaurant was without lights because of the flood in Tubarao. We heard customers around us complained to the waiter that the meat was too salty. The other nine of us said nothing but wanted to cry that those in Tubarao would not even have that.

At the Airport – No Vacancies on the Plane

Finally, the pickup left us at the airport. There I was bare foot. In the same clothes I had worn for five days. Three little children, and a muddy suitcase. And they tell me there were no available seats on the last plane out that day for Sao Paulo! They had heard about the flood in our city and were sympathetic.

I stood with my little group on the airstrip while the plane loaded. We were wet and cold. Numb. And maybe I showed it because a stranger took me a chair to the airstrip to use as we waited.

Now I was sitting in the middle of the airstrip with my little group huddled against me. Waiting. I was thinking. "Father, You take it from here. You know where we are, from where we have come, and when we need to leave here. You are my strength, because I don't seem to have much of my own."

Someone was giving us a signal to go to the plane. They had arranged two seats for the four of us and it was a luxury for us after an eight-hour trip in the rain in the back of a pickup. Passengers looked around at us, and some finally asked if there were any connections of our plight with the flood.

I smiled and teased, "What gave us away?"

It was the first good laugh we had experienced, and what needed medicine it was. For the rest of the flight, they listened as I told of God's grace and protection to our group and the great challenge that was facing the city of Tubarao.

There were even North Americans on the plane. Two business people from Kansas trapped in Tubarão. A Rotary exchange student from California. It seemed they were understanding my testimony in Portuguese. I hope so.

Plane, Bus, Taxi, and Car Ride with Strangers

in Sao Paulo

We finally arrived in Congonhas Airport in Sao Paulo. I felt a little sorry for people who tried not to stare. I carried Tania and the muddy suitcase, bare footed, with little Kemper and Cindy holding to my skirt tail.

Next came a bus ride to the city of Campinas, then a taxi ride, and a car ride with strangers. Since I had snatched up my purse as we fled from our house that Saturday night, I had the keys to the mission hospitality apartment in Campinas. A very nice couple gave us a ride up to the door of the apartment. The feeling was indescribable!

Solid dry ground. Water to drink. A telephone. Electricity. A bath! Praise to God who brought us that far.

Inside, the first item on the list was a bath for the children. However, as I turned on the electric shower head (which heated the water) it blew a fuse, the water turned cold, and we were in the dark again. I dressed the children and marched them up three flights of stairs to see if a certain Christian couple happened to still live there. They were home.

I knocked on their door. When a young man answered I introduced myself and explained our condition.

"Why, we just now saw the news on television about Tubarao and were wishing we could help in some way. And here you are at our door!" he exclaimed.

He went down the three flights of stairs with us to the apartment where he replaced the burned fuse and reminded us to turn out all excess lights before we turned on the electric shower head again!

"Have you eaten anything?" he asked.

"We all had orange juice," I said.

"You go ahead and take care of the children", he suggested, "and I will be back."

Soon the neighbor returned and he was certainly welcomed by the children. He brought a whole baked chicken and a long fresh slim Brazilian bread. When we started to cut the bread, the center was empty. Three-year-old Tania had pulled out the soft part of the bread up to her elbow. Who could blame her?

It has remained etched in our memory for many years – the taste, the smell, and the feeling. It was the taste and smell of food and the feeling of the attention of our friend and the goodness of God. I remember. I pray for them. I wish I could remember their names.

Wednesday night. March 27

At last, I could telephone fellow missionaries in Brazil, the General Director Reford Wilson in Nashville, Tennessee, and our families in the USA.

First Days of a New Future

Remember that I was still without shoes. A Brazilian friend sent me some shoes. Fellow missionaries, Sam and June Wilkinson took the children and me *to Evangelandia* campground in Jaboticabal, Sao Paulo where we spent the next month in one of the dorms.

News reports reached us that over 3,000 died and of the 12,000 homes in Tubarao, 3,000 had been completely destroyed with 7,000 more seriously damaged. Agriculture was reported to be a total loss. Government officials said it would take up to ten years to restore the town. However, there was no way they could calculate the spirit of the people in the future restoration.

Soon Sam and Ivan Lopes loaded a Volks van with shovels, flashlights, personal hygiene items (like toilet tissue), clothing, and even writing material. After the two-day journey, the two men arrived in the city where both had lived before to search for Jim among the ruins.

They found him! What a greeting. Together they distributed the goods they had brought for flood survivors. Not one person from our Bible study group lost his or her life. Great news and celebration.

On the way back to Jaboticabal, Jim shared the incredible stories from families connected with our prayer groups regarding their close calls with death. The city government was asking those who remained in the city to move out while order was being restored. We were scheduled to return to the USA in a few months for our regular state-side assignment, so an early departure seemed to be an answer.

Our people in Tubarao understood but they hated to see us leave. Soon most of them were also scattered to various places trying to restructure their lives.

The testimony of one man encouraged us.

"I'm not angry with God," he said. "The Bible studies in your home helped me to accept all this. There were 45 of us in the rafters of a falling coffee mill with water all around. As we had learned at your house, we prayed for God to save us. He did! Please come to our house and have services every chance you get once all this gets back to normal."

Yes. God called us to Martinho Ghizzo Street, house number 57, and allowed us to pass through the experience. Two years later he called us right back to the same street, the same, but restored, house. He continued to be the same God.

We pray we won't soon forget it. And we still pack up when he says, "Move on!"

We know that "here we have no continuing city, but we seek one to come". Hebrews 13:14

Chapter Six

Second State-Side Assignment – USA-1974

We were so pleased to see the American flag waving at the Tulsa International Airport when we arrived. After the flood, we went to Oklahoma for our State-side assignment. On Carlsbad Street in Owasso, Oklahoma, three of my siblings and some nieces had bought houses from a brother-in-law. So did we.

We chose not to home school our children while in the USA. We enrolled Kemper in the third grade and Cindy in the first grade at Barnes Elementary school in Owasso. At that time parents felt safe in turning their children over to public schools to teach basic truth to their children.

We especially enjoyed being at my home church in Owasso with preaching, praise and worship in English when we were not traveling.

Cindy

We traveled to churches who had sent us to Brazil and gave reports with our thanks. Once Jim went to California without the family for their month-long mission conference. Our second child, Cindy, was about six-years-old and watching television in our living room with Kemper and Tania. It was a novelty since we hadn't had one yet in Brazil.

She tearfully looked at me and said, "I wish Daddy were an ape!"

"An ape, sweetheart? Why?" I asked, trying to understand. That's when I noticed they were watching the film, Planet of the Apes.

"If he were an ape, then I could at least see him on television." The children missed their father.

Later she was listening to a gospel record for children. It was a story about a little boy who hid a baby poisonous snake against his mother's advice. Billy thought he could hide it in a box without anyone knowing about it. It grew up and escaped from the box and one day it killed his dog. It ended up biting Billy. His mother cut a cross over the bite and sucked out the poison. His mother told him about the cross of Jesus and how much Jesus loved him. Billy admitted he was wrong and decided to obey his mother and follow Jesus, too.

Cindy was really impressed.

She ran into the room where I was and said, "Mama, I need to pray and get saved."

"Okay, honey, we can do that now."

"Billy hid his sins about the snake and I need to ask forgiveness and get saved, too."

We knelt beside the bed as she prayed her prayer of repentance. As soon as she finished, she said, "Let's call Daddy in California and tell him." Jim had been gone for four weeks in missionary conferences.

"I want Daddy to help Brother Pirtle baptize me." So as soon as her father returned to Oklahoma, she was baptized at the FW Baptist church in Owasso. The heater had gone out of the baptistery on that cold day in October and at first, she was hesitant when they told her. But she was determined to be baptized anyway!

She grew up in Brazil, attended the *Semionario Batista Livre* in Ribeirao Preto, Hillsdale Free Will Baptist College in Oklahoma, and then returned to Brazil to graduate from *Faculdade Sao Luis*. She married a Brazilian from the church who was studying law. She is now a mother of Jonathan, Julia, and David.

She learned to play the flute, helped teach at youth camps, and was very helpful in the children's home, *Lar Nova Vida*. She taught at *the Brazilian Bible College,* too.

At this writing Cindy is working at a bank. She has also worked in insurance, real estate, and the Oklahoma Department of Human Services.

A Surprise Gift-ACC

While still on state-side-assignment, we received an invitation to be Directors of Student Activities at the American Christian College on Sheridan Avenue in Tulsa. The College placed emphasis on patriotism and citizenship. Its president was Dr. David A. Noebel. Faculty, Staff, and students were blessings.

The city of Tubarao was not restored yet to receive the return of its citizens so we moved to the college. It was like a gift of God while we waited to return to our beloved Brazil.

We moved our family one more time. We placed our children in the Hoover Grade School nearby. Kemper got to be in the

Cub Scouts and Cindy in the Brownie Scouts. They adjusted quickly and enjoyed the freedom of riding their bike and playing on campus. Little Tania followed us around while her siblings were in school.

We lived in the dormitory and our apartment was one of the favorite meeting places for our dear students. We spent hours listening, praying, serving snacks, helping with theme parties, and the yearbook. They were really a fine group of young people from all over the USA and from other countries.

The sweetest memories were that they called us "Mom and "Dad'. They put in the yearbook this description:

"On furlough from the mission field of Brazi Mr. and Mrs.

Combs came to ACC to fill the role of Directors of Student

Activities. From inspecting dorms,   to issuing late passes,

to consoling broken hearts, and nursing the flu epidemic

they kept on the run, but they always had time to be

everywhere with everyone and spread their love to all in

their large campus family. "

Our young children were favorites to the students who were far from their families. The students included them in their sports activities, their special events, and nightly devotions.

They were a novelty being bi-lingual and attracted the international students. As I mentioned, ACC was a gift from God at our waiting time. Go Crusaders!!

At the same time, Jim graduated with his Master's Degree from Tulsa University and I finished the hours I needed to finish my Bachelor's Degree. (I received my MRS degree, first) We also had freedom to keep in touch with our supporting churches.

We finally had the green light to return to Tubarao.

Chapter Seven

Third Term In Brazil

1976-Return to Tubarao

We sold our house in Owasso and we returned to Martinho Ghuizzo Street, 57, where we bought the same house in Tubarão we had rented before the flood. It had been restored as had the houses around us where many of the folks lived who attended our house church group.

The city of Tubarao was stronger than anyone had judged and had returned to livable conditions years before it was predicted. Most of our friends had returned to the city, but we had all changed in some ways after what we had been through. We were where God wanted us to be and we were ready to join forces to continue to partner with God in Shark City.

As the group gathered back together and brought others, it outgrew our house church. We needed to find another meeting place. Families that moved back had lost many of their things so they started again with the bare minimum.

Remodeled House for the Group

We were able to purchase a simple two-bedroom wood frame house on the same block as our home. We tore down walls and the men built a pulpit, benches and a small raised stage.

Jim built a concrete tank with steps leading down into it in the front yard near a weeping willow and palm trees. It was ready for the next baptisms.

The youth attracted the youth and we took them on bus trips to youth camps two states above us to Evangelandia, Jaboticabal. Then two states below us to youth camp near the border of Uruguay and Brazil. They learned to read their Bible and pray and seemed to embrace the Good News. The parents of some were fine with all that, but when it came to baptism, they drew the line.

Their children had been baptized at infancy and it was a symbol to the parents that they were choosing one faith and rejecting another. Well, that is exactly what the Bible teaches that baptism is about, surrendering your all to the Lord Jesus. We taught that where the Scriptures teach to "believe and be baptized", the person should be old enough to "believe". We explained that we dedicated children to the Lord as Mary and Joseph did baby Jesus, but knew the person one day should choose to accept salvation in the risen Lord.

We also taught that we did not want them to be baptized behind their parents' back or without their blessings. Three never received the blessings while we were there. They became nurses and a dentist. I pray one day as adults they made the decision themselves. I love them so much.

In our little church building we also offered free English classes. We had some children of government workers, students and teachers, and a doctor. His nickname was Dr. Leprinho, because he took care of patients with leprosy.

A couple arrived one night at church. They were Christians looking for an evangelical group. Sr. Matos was a musician and ended up playing the guitar and leading our choir.

Another family was Sr. Claro, his wife, and his teenage children. They had an office and school supply store in their home which we visited. They were a great addition to our church and to our family.

Tania

Our own child, Tania, was one of the first to be baptized in the new baptistery. One Sunday night she told me,

'*Mamae, quero aceitar Cristo hoje a noite na igreja."*

"How wonderful. You don't have to wait until tonight to accept Christ, you know."

"Oh, I want to wait until tonight at church, *Mamae."*

That night she sat close to me and reminded me what she had planned to do. After a while I noticed just how quiet she was – she was asleep!

"Oh, well," I mused, "she is only seven and she must accept Christ when she is ready."

At the end of the closing hymn, she woke up and looked around. Her father was saying the benediction.

"*Mamae,"* she tugged at my skirt, "I'm supposed to accept Jesus and get saved tonight."

"You went to sleep, sweetheart. You can do it at home," I comforted her.

"No, I want to do it here and tonight."

She walked up to the front and knelt down at the altar her grandfather had made on his last trip to Brazil. I whispered to Jim what had happened and he called the people who were visiting to order.

'What is Tania doing" they were asking.

Our Brazilian Christians had made decisions in their home and since it was a new work, they had never seen anyone kneel at the altar in a church before. Since Tania had been born in Brazil, we couldn't remember where she had seen it done that way. But as she arose from the altar, our tiny blond-haired daughter had tears streaming from her blue-green eyes. Many other brown eyes were swimming with tears, also.

Tania was baptized in the outside baptistery under the banana trees along with other Brazilians.

She grew up in Brazil, then attended Hillsdale Free Will Baptist College (now Randall University) in Oklahoma, where she received her A.A. degree, and then went on to the University of Central Oklahoma where she received B.A. in business.

She has a special gift in music – voice and guitar- and was part of choir groups in college and in church and camps.

Many times, her bedroom made room for active little girls who were curious about her fair skin, the color of barriga *de peixe* (fish's belly), and admired her willingness to share her home and parents with them.

She was a bi-lingual secretary to the president of the SONOCO FORPLAS Company in Araras. She also worked in the business office at Hillsdale. At this writing she works at FAA (Federal Aviation Administration) in the Radar business offices. We call her our international hostess. She and her husband open their home for church and family reunions where it is common to have several languages represented. She and her husband are now grandparents with a new generation to guide into a love for Jesus.

Can a child find forgiveness and salvation in Jesus Christ? Oh, yes! And that is our main source of hope for suffering, wounded children all over the world who have not really had a chance to be children.

Satan wants to destroy our children. That has been his tactic since the first murder among young brothers.

Pharaoh ordered the Hebrew babies to be killed.

Herod ordered the slaughter of babies.

Pagan and cultic groups use babies in their sacrifices.

What tactic is Satan using in our beloved United States and other countries? The murder of infants called Abortion.

Yes, a child can be used by Satan and filled with evil, but God crated us to be filled with His love and His Spirit! We must desire life, spiritual life for today's children.

"Even a child is known by his doing, whether his work be pure, and whether it be right." Proverbs 20:11

Mosquito Escape

Since we were south of the equator, December was in the middle of hot summer. In November we had started practicing

---

a Christmas drama and Cantata. They were very talented in memorizing and drama and rehearsals were a bonding time. Everyone was enthusiastic. But the week before Christmas we saw our neighbors packing up to go to the beach. Several even packed up their kitchen stove (which ran on little tank of propane). They said everyone always leaves before Christmas to camp at the beach to get away from the heat and mosquitoes.

Uh oh. We checked on those attending our church and they had left town, also. Our city was about 20 minutes from the beach. We had never lived near beaches. There are none in our area of Sao Paulo, nor in Oklahoma and West Virginia.

You can believe we were better prepared for the Christmas season during the next years. So, what did we do? We took our Christmas and summer evangelism to the beach.

One of the families in our group had been hit hard by the flood and had a large family of 11. They were desperate to sell a rustic three-room beach house. We were able to buy it at a good price to use for beach evangelism

Summer Evangelism

We arranged the tiny rustic wooden beach house with an outdoor toilet and outdoor faucet. It had a detached wooden garage so we got busy making some changes.

Some of the guys helped and we added piped water into the tiny kitchen, and an indoor bathroom. The shower was in the backyard.

Jim and the men remodeled the garage with triple high bunk beds on the back wall. These were for volunteers who would be helping in the evangelism. We invited some other missionary friends to help with the summer evangelism. The first to use the garage were missionaries Dub and Marcia Ellison and children who slept on the bunks. Two rooms in the beach house were only large enough for a wall-to-wall bed. The Wilkinson family and our family slept there. Ivan and Rubens, musicians from Jaboticabal, slept in the Wilkinson's car.

On the side walls of the garage, Jim had made benches that could be lifted on hinges and fastened to the wooden walls after the meetings. We had afternoon child evangelism classes for the children in the garage. However, it was too small for the evening meetings so we put up a white sheet on the outside of the garage and showed films on a 16 mm movie projector as the crowd stood. Guitars and singing echoed throughout the beach.

We sang songs we had taught the children in the afternoon. During those years, TV reception was difficult at the beach and there were very few. Once the sun went down, entertainment for the other beach dwellers took place on their front porches where the temperature dropped each night. Table games, music with guitars and accordions, and conversations were the nightly routine.

Our evening activities were a novelty for the beach community, and each night the attendance increased. Praise God.

We got fresh drinking water from on top of the hill. Other water was boiled before using. We kept several pressure cookers going to feed the young, hungry group of volunteers who really worked hard, played hard, and made lifelong friends. A few of the locals had accepted Christ and others carried the evangelism seed with them.

Yes, we still had Christmas dramas and cantatas in years to come, but we presented them before we escaped to the beach to avoid the heat and mosquitos.

In 1979 my parents visited us in Tubarao to celebrate their 50th Wedding Anniversary. Our Brazilian church people were so gracious to them and prepared a beautiful celebration for their special date. My folks did not speak Portuguese and the people did not speak English but they worked and laughed side by side.

My father, with his pastor's heart, said before leaving,

'If I could speak this language, I would like to come here and help build churches." He also enjoyed the year-round supply of watermelon!

It was so good for them to see where God had taken their children they had surrendered to His will. They had prepared me from a child to surrender to God's will and they were very supportive of missionaries.

One of the family had told me that mother confessed that when I told them that God had called me to be a missionary, she wanted to scream. But she knew that if that was what God wanted, then if Marie was the thing standing in the way, God could take Marie out of the picture in order to clear the way. So, she wisely surrendered to God's will and supported her daughter even though it was very painful to let her go.

So those days in Brazil they could see the fruit of their surrender embracing them and thanking them for sending their daughter to them. It was a balm to their souls. And to mine.

Tearful Departure

Near the end of our term, the Brazil Field Council of FWB Missionaries requested we return to the state of Sao Paulo. The Wilkinson's left for State-side Assignment and a family was needed to direct camps at Evangelandia in Jaboticabal and to work with the church until the Jim Cowart family finished Language School in Campinas.

"The harvest is plentiful, but the laborers are few; therefore, pray earnestly to the Lord of the harvest to send out laborers into his harvest." Matthew 9:37-38

What a decision. We did pray earnestly to the Lord. Two needy places. Jim presented to the Field Council the possibility of someone making the long bus trip to Tubarao at least once a month to assist the new converts there. They agreed. We sold everything and left.

For the next year Jim was the only one to go back to Tubarao. He traveled one full day there and another day back. (like Oklahoma to California) and preached the weekend in their homes.

Beautiful Evangelandia

The Evangelandia mission camp ground needed a lot of maintenance, but it was beautiful. Tropical trees. Three dorm buildings, cafeteria, and the ever-popular *cantina*. Palm trees. Pine trees. Fruit trees. Flowers of many kinds and colors.

Soccer field, basketball court, ping pong room, and an open tabernacle with many memories of lives transformed and leaders called to ministry. (And over dozen toilet stools to prepare before each camp.)

I am a great believer in family camps and youth camps. We had the minimum of five a year and I was involved in all of them, and loved it. I would write the literature for the leaders, train them, make music and scripture posters, prepare menus, and prepare for the cleaning before and after each camp. Then I would teach the nationals to do the same in the following years Yes, it was worth it. We were there for a short time, but we would return again a few years later.

It was a beautiful place for ministry, but it was a great place to rear our children. We home schooled them in English and they also went to Brazilian public school in Portuguese .Jim home schooled Cindy, and I home schooled Tania and Kemper. A wonderful experience.

They had space to play and ride their bikes in nature filled surroundings. We inherited watch dogs when we moved there and they always had lots of puppies. One had 11 at one time so we named them January to November.

The Church

For the short time we were there, we enjoyed working with the church members. Rubinho had already been to the beach to help us out in summer evangelism. He was a musician who played, sang, and composed music. He and other young people were very active and soon became family. They were at our home a lot and it gave time for discipleship.

The Cowart's moved on the camp ground as soon as they finished language school. Jim, Karen, and their first two children, Mark and Melissa (Missy), were warmly welcomed by the church.

Another Invitation – Another Good-bye

We received an invitation from Hillsdale Free Will Baptist College in Oklahoma (Now Randall University) to head up the Missions Department. Bro Reford Wilson had resigned and soon passed away. It was the end of our term and we accepted after conferring with the Foreign Mission Department. They gave us their blessing.

Although it was a great opportunity to serve, it was still an unexpected change of what I felt was a career missionary commitment. I confess that I shed a few tears, but then the Lord showed me that it was an opportunity to multiply myself if we could see young people surrendering to mission work and young pastors leading their people to obey the Great Commission. With that peace we packed and left for Oklahoma.

When we arrived at the Tulsa International Airport for our third State-Side Assignment, my Roberts family as well as Jim's sister, Judy, and her husband, Jim , were there to meet us. They were living in Moore at that time. It was our daughter Cindy's 12th birthday, May 28, 1980.

After we visited with family and our main supporters in the area, we moved our family to the campus.

Chapter Eight

New Assignment In the USA -1980

Another Campus – Hillsdale (Randall University)

The College had an apartment prepared for our family of five on one end of a dormitory. We enrolled the children in Moore Schools. One more address for our family at 3701 S. I-35 Service Road. It was a happy meeting place for Missionary Kids from Brazil, Kevin Wilkinson, Kenan Wilkinson, Andrew Eagleton, and also our niece Becky Combs, and Jim's youngest brother, Scot Combs from West Virginia.

Missions and Students

We were pleased to see that the College was still faithful in emphasizing the Great Commission of Jesus to take the Good News to all the world.

Prayer Band and Foreign Missions Fellowship were two important branches of Student Life that worked well together. Prayer Band consisted of students who had a compassion for lost souls, a concern for the mission fields, and willingness to pray diligently for missionary needs. The group met each day to discuss these needs, share praise items, and pray for each request. Each day represented a different field and need.

Foreign Mission Fellowship met monthly to discuss foreign mission situations and to help plan the annual Missionary

Conference in the Fall, a missions retreat in the Spring, and fund-raising activity projects.

Mission Conferences

Jim and I taught missions classes, supported the prayer bands, and Foreign Mission Fellowship, but the Missions Conference each year was one of the highlights for me. To introduce the students to testimonies of the fruit of sharing salvation in Jesus Christ to every tribe and nation around the world.

From 1980 to 1985 they had on their campus National and International missionaries at the Mission Conferences. Representing National Missions were: Richard Kennedy from California, Paul Thompson from Arizona, Jimmy Smith from Weatherford, Oklahoma.

Representing International Missions were: Dale and Sandra Bishop, Judy Smith, and Jerry Banks from Japan. Sherwood Lee, Archie Mayhew, Eddie Payne, Howard Filkins from Ivory Coast, West Africa. Paul Robinson from Uruguay. Earnie and Willie Jean Deeds, and the Combs from Brazil.

Another couple, Oklahoma alumni from Hillsdale, was there to challenge the students to answer the call of God to go where He directs. John and Kay Metcalf were so talented. They were missionary appointees to Brazil, but a tragic automobile accident took their lives right before they were to leave. Without knowing, their mission was to challenge others to go, to obey. There is a dormitory at Evangelandia Camp Ground in Brazil holding a plaque showing METCALF DORM. Built by FWB Master's Men organization sent there to honor the young couple who said 'Yes" to God.

Student Response

It was encouraging when we saw our students responding to opportunities to see firsthand the tremendous need and the great opportunities to partner with God to spread the Gospel.

They went to France, Panama, Ivory Coast, Japan, and Brazil as student missionaries during school vacations. Some went on to apply for career missionary status and others became mission minded pastors and church members who promote sending and praying for those who go.

We had student missionaries in our home in Brazil from Welch College and Randall University to work with us who are now on our missionary maps, serving God.

Young people sitting in the student chairs later went on to be directly involved in missions: Lila Nichols, Curt and Mary Holland, Brad Ransom, Earnest Holland, and Mark Brashier. What an honor to have invested in these lives!

Two More Addresses

Jim received an invitation to be the Chaplain to 900 residents of the Lexington Prison. I continued to teach at the College, but we moved our family to a home at 1700 Rock Hallow in Moore. During the summer I had a lump removed from my left breast. God and my in-laws, the Puckett's, were there with us.

At the same time Jim was working at the prison, the Dibble Free Will Baptist Church called him to pastor there. We moved our family to a mobile home on the Dibble Camp Ground. I continued to teach at the College and drove to Moore.

Small communities and small schools have their advantages. At the moment of this writing, statistics show Dibble has a population of 870 and 645 students.

Our children blossomed with the opportunities in the church and school there. Some of the teachers and administrators were from our church and other churches from there. Our home-schooled children fit in well scholastically with the public system. They were on the honor rolls and in the advanced classes. The girls were cheer-leaders and Kemper was Vice-President of the Student Council. We were in Dibble long enough for Kemper to graduate from high school there. Go 1984 graduates!! He enrolled as a freshman at Hillsdale Free Will Baptist College in Moore and lived on campus.

Amazing sisters from the church, Janet and Jaunice, did wonders in including our children in the dramas, Vacation Bible School, youth camps and music. Their husbands were deacons and great help to Jim and their children soon found a special place in our hearts. So many wonderful forever friends from the church.

The school was right across from our Free Will Baptist Church. We could do pastoral visitation by attending the Friday night sports events because most of the church members and families were there!

We had been in the United States for four years and our parents visited us in Dibble and saw God working there. However, they didn't say anything to us, but personally were wondering if we shouldn't go back to Brazil where the need was also so great.

Years later I heard that Jim's father talked to him at a National Convention about returning to Brazil. Later Bro. Cecil preached at Dibble Church about Jonah. *Pronto!* That was it. Jim talked to me about it and then to the International Mission Board. Me? I was ready. Kemper would continue at Hillsdale College and the girls would go with us.

Once again, we sold our house and were packing to follow God's will for our family.

Chapter Nine

Fourth Term in Brazil

Back to Brazil –Ribeirao Preto - 1985

The Brazilian Field Council of Missionaries asked us to move to Ribeirao Preto where the missionary Bobby Poole had been working. So, we moved there and assumed some of their projects, too. They were very talented and hardworking missionaries.

We helped in two churches which kept all of us busy. We took over some of their projects. I edited the small magazine in Portuguese called *Folha Evangelica* and offered the Source of Light Correspondence Courses in Portuguese.

The correspondence courses added up to about 100 envelopes per week. We had more than 500 students enrolled, up 300 from the year before. We offered three different courses totaling 22 lessons. We checked the lessons and recorded the grades on file cards. There were no computers at that time.

Sometimes a letter would contain a testimony and a decision for Christ. One of us would say, "I got a decision!" and then we would sit down and read. Translating from Portugues is one example we found:

"I was involved in so much sin and rebellion that I was breaking my parents' hearts. They are religious Catholics, but couldn't give me answers. A friend invited me to a Protestant church and gave me a coupon to study this course."

Another one wrote, "I passed a group singing in the *praca* and stopped to listen. One guy told how God freed him from drugs and I knew I had the same problem. I accepted Christ, and your Bible study course has helped me grow in the Lord."

Our students represented ten Brazilian States. One day, to our surprise, we opened a letter from a man in a Portuguese speaking country in Africa. Laborers are few and we couldn't go to all these states, but the Word of God was going in these many envelopes we sent each week.

A New Family Member

But we had a responsibility to take the Word locally. At the mission church in the Ipiranga neighborhood, we were reaching several families. There are many stories, but I can give you one example. Two young boys went one Easter Sunday morning hoping to get a chocolate egg we were passing out after the service. Sebastião and Marco Antonio. They ended up accepting Christ as Savior later and were baptized by Jim in the little baptistery revealed by lifting a door in the floor of the tiny stage at the front of the mission church.

Marco Antonio's parents lived in an abandoned shack. We heard that his father had burned Marco's Bible and clothes. One Sunday morning he didn't show up for church. Unusual for him. Jim had obligations in the other church that day, so I asked one of the young leaders, Caesar, a veterinarian, to go with me to Marcos' house after church.

When we got to the shanty and entered into the dark room, the boy was standing by his mother in the only chair in the room. Blood was running down her neck from a gash in the back of her ear.

We introduced ourselves and explained that we were from the church. Marco Antonio didn't show up today and we were concerned. Maybe we can help with something.

His father turned away from us and looked toward the wall. "That boy comes in here talking about strange religions. He took my gods off the shelf and broke and burned them."

"We heard you burned his Bible and his clothes. Can you tell me why you did that," I quietly asked.

"A curse! That's what that Bible is. Ever since he brought that Book into this house only evil has come to us." His voice was rising and arms swinging. I moved to stand between him and Marco. "He should be bringing in things for us, for me. All he thinks about is himself and that church, so I burned his clothes and everything else."

Caesar calmly and lovingly told the beautiful story of the gospel, and it had never sounded so hopeful, as simple and as powerful as it did in that setting of darkness. He moved over to the woman and checked the head wound on the woman. We left with a promise to see him that night, but I was never able to forget that scene. That scene influenced personal decisions and personal commitments we would face in the future.

We learned that Marco Antonio was sneaking in the back of the church and sleeping in the bathroom because his father sent him away. Well, you guessed it. We took him home with us. We arranged a birth certificate for him so that he could go to school. His mother didn't know his birthdate so Marco Antonio chose a holiday. He learned to read and write. Lived together with our own children and we gave him the responsibility of helping with correspondence courses. He was just learning to read but he could stuff the envelopes, and take the correspondence to the downtown post office. He and Sebastião helped at the Ipiranga church.

They are all grown now. Marco Antonio married a fine Christian girl, has four children, is an ordained preacher and is pastoring a church right now.

Our children paid his way to Oklahoma to see their father before he changed his address to heaven, and he sang at his funeral a song in Portuguese. *"Milagre Sou"* (I Am a Miracle) He is an example of what missions is all about. Transforming a life to be used of Christ to win others.

Ribeirao Preto is a large city with missionary families from different denominations. They had joined together their home-schooled Missionary Kids to meet in one of the churches using one of our FWB missionaries as the monitor, Vickie Sturgill.

They used a homeschool course especially for missionary families that we were familiar with.

It was good that the girls were not studying by themselves, but studying at home did not include a uniform which they "got tired of". Cindy finished high school there in 1986 as the only senior. She said that at least she could claim to be Valedictorian!

Wayne moved His Address to Heaven

During this term I made a trip home for my only brother's funeral/home going. He died of cancer at the age of 57. The family asked me to do his eulogy at the celebration of his life.

He was a deacon in the church, and played the guitar and led singing. He was a high school math teacher and Shop teacher. Then he became a lieutenant in the Tulsa County Sheriff Department. Mother mentioned that police work was dangerous and he said if a Christian shouldn't be in police work, who should?

Many friends and family gathered at Rejoice FWB church where Bro. Leonard Pirtle did a good job leading the service.

Wayne loved his cowboy boots and attire and maybe he will be able to wear white boots in heaven, who knows?

Another Move to Evangelandia

When the Poole's returned from State Side Assignment, the Field Council asked us to move to Jaboticabal to prepare the church for a Brazilian Pastor and take care of the Camp ministries.

The field council started a Seminary on campus and we had several fine young men and women and faculty living there. We just all merged as family.

One of my large projects was setting up the library for the students from donated books by generous Christians.

Many hours of hands-on labeling and cataloging, but it was worth it.

I continued writing, designing, and printing Bible lessons in Portuguese for Vacation Bible Schools while living at Evangelandia camp grounds. At that time, we could not buy them at Christian Book Stores and we needed them to train our Brazilians to carry on their own ministries.

Our new address was Camp Evangelandia again. We were involved with many camps again as well as the church until Brazillian Pastor Jeancarlo and wife Flavia came. Our children were older and helped in the church. Tania and Flavia played guitars in the praise band and Cindy taught classes in youth camps. They both have beautiful singing voices.

I offered free English conversational classes to some scientist/professor at the Jaboticabal Agricultural College. I used flannel graph figures on the Life of Christ. One was especially interested in the genealogy chart on the life of Christ. One had a doctorate on the membrane of the egg! They were also looking at cloning in the 80's. They met in the library of the Seminary on campus. That caused them to ask questions about the doctrines of the Bible and the outreach of a Protestant church.

It was the end of our term and the church was in the good hands of the young couple, Jeancarlo and Flavia Ache. So once again we packed our things and flew back to Oklahoma.

Chapter Ten

Fourth Assignment in USA – 1989

Noble, Oklahoma

My sister, Dolores Shivers, invited us to make her home our headquarters while we were traveling over the country. So, we unloaded our things and moved in to her home at 604 Eighth Street, in Noble. Her home had two full apartments upstairs and she opened both for us, free of charge. It was a blessing to be able to open our bags and ministry materials and to contact our next appointments. And it was so good to catch up on family news.

She had been attending the Free Will Baptist church in Norman since 1970 when her children were ten and eight. They used their big home to entertain the youth, the young couples, and their Sunday School Class. Her children are adults now and their families still attend the church. Now called Crosspointe FWB Church, in Norman.

Since she worked each day at an upscale men's store in Norman, Harry Holshers, we practically had the house to ourselves when we were not on the road. To show our gratitude we prepared hot meals for her to come home to. We enjoyed visiting together around an Okie menu of beans, fried potatoes, fried okra, cornbread, and ice tea. Of course, we also introduced her to Brazilian dishes.

Before we left for the USA, I had received an invitation from Dr. Thomas Marberry to return to Hillsdale FWB College (now Randall University) to help in the mission's department again. We discussed that Jim could travel to the supporting church and friends and I would go with him when the places were close by and during school vacation.

My custom was to go to the Bible to help in decisions, and this was a BIG one. I just couldn't find the peace on this decision so I went to my Bible reading. I was in the book of Ecclesiastes. I thought maybe it would say "that which is to be has already been" or there is a "time for everything". Or something. I really loved to teach and loved the times we were there before. Encouraging students, pastors, and missionary candidates. But I always looked forward to visiting with supporters to hear how their investments brought fruit for God's glory.

Let me share my daily reading from Ecclesiastes that day.
"Two are better than one; because they have a good reward for their labor. For if they fall, the one will lift up his fellow: but woe to him that is alone when he falls; for he had not another to help him up. Again, if two lie together, then they have heat; but how can one be warm alone?" Ec. 4:9-11

Well, I phoned and thanked Dr. Marberry before we left Brazil and quoted these verses. I had peace about deciding not to teach at the college and to go with Jim on deputation. But I had no idea how true the verses would be.

Flat on the Pews

Somewhere in traveling from coast to coast, from church to church, Jim started suffering terrific back pain.

At each church I took the display and literature from the trunk of the car, and set it up in the church. Jim lay down on a pew until time for the service to begin. By that time the pastor, or whoever was in charge, noticed his problem, but Jim wanted to continue with the service. It was very good each time. God's mercy carried us through.

After the service, he was in great pain and after the folks left, he lay down on a pew again while I took down the display. Usually, someone would help me carry everything to the car. We always had a tight schedule and needed to get on the road.

The scriptures came alive for us. If one falls, the other one will be there to lift him up. I was glad I could be there to help him. With God's help we finished our schedule for a while and went back to Noble. We took out a short time for Jim to have back surgery and he recovered quickly. (I remembered the other scripture, too, when he let me warm my cold toes on his warm body! Verse 11)

Jim visited his folks in West Virginia. His father was pastoring and his mother, Norma, wasn't well, but they sent us back to Brazil with their blessings.

After the end of our year in the USA, we made plans to return to Brazil. We had a daughter engaged and we needed to get back to Araras!

Chapter Eleven

Fifth Term in Brazil – 1990

Araras, Sao Paulo

We moved back to our home at Morada do Sol. We had three churches at that time and the next four years brought changes for our family and for the ministry in our city.

Mamaw's New Address

One day we were in Campinas, about an hour away from our home in Araras. We had stopped by the mission apartment when the phone rang. It was a message from Jim's family in West Virginia. His sweet mother, Norma Elisabeth Ball Combs, had moved her address to heaven.

Mother of 15, a pastor's wife, a great home maker who knew how to delegate, was known as a great cook and generous woman of Christian hospitality. She liked to pull her chair in front of the TV, place her ball cap on her head, and root for her favorite baseball team. And maybe sneak a few chocolates covered cherries. She didn't drive, but loved to shop when someone could drive her.

She also did all that while giving herself daily injections for her diabetes. Amazing mother.

A family member, Robbie Combs, offered to fly his own plane to take Jim home for the funeral. Since he had just seen her before returning to Brazil, he chose not to return. When he hung up the phone, he broke down and wept. He said that he thought he was prepared for that news but he was surprised at how hard he was hit. So difficult to be so far away at that time.

His family loved and respected him and I felt his family needed him at that time, but I didn't say anything. We just held hands together for a moment then went home to tell our children that their Mamaw had moved to another address – heaven. What a comfort to tell them that they could see her again one day.

Wedding Feast for 300

That same year our daughter, Cindy, was married in the church in Araras where she was dedicated to the Lord as an infant. The young man, Jose Augusto de Aquino, was from one of our churches. Friends from all the addresses we had lived before and one friend from Kentucky, 'Uncle' Richard Howard, were there. Missionaries in Brazil, Jim and Vickie Sturgil, were part of her ceremony. Jim, her father, performed the ceremony. Kemper would be returning in just a few days to the USA so he and Tania were there to help their sister and brother-in-law celebrate.

The custom in Brazil was to give a big banquet for the wedding party after the ceremony. Jim wanted to prepare 'churrasco', a Brazilian type of grilling many types of meat, for 300 people! Some ladies from the church and I prepared buckets of small whole seasoned potatoes. They said it was typical at weddings, but I didn't prepare them for our next two wedding feasts! Plenty of rice with garlic and onions. We rented a place, decorated it, and had a great time of photos and celebration.

At that time in the USA the weddings and receptions were still in the church with cake, punch, mints and mixed nuts.

Wow, that has really changed!

Surprise at City Hall

One day Margarida, a school teacher from our church, and I were in City Hall to represent our small church. The church was excited about their multi-ministry efforts in the neighborhood and felt they could do more for the community.

Since the church had teachers, nurses, business people, and other professionals as members, some suggested we consider opening a free Christian day care center in a poor neighborhood. We were there at city hall to check about the most strategic location in the city for the center.

We were in for a surprise.

Dona Olga, the director of the Department of Human services, was also the mother of a young man attending our church. She heard our offer and responded,

"Araras is a model city for day care centers. We have some new, modern centers that aren't even full yet. Would you consider doing something else for the community?"

I looked at Margarida then said, "We had mentioned the possibility of working with the elderly or my husband had mentioned work with street children in the future..."

"That's it,' she interrupted, "we have a great need for someone to work with street children. We have children sniffing glue. We have children giving birth to children and giving drugs to their babies. These children are in the streets begging, forming gangs and stealing, especially from downtown shops. They are abused and beaten at home so they flee to the streets for their entertainment, education and what they think is safety."

My heart seemed to be thudding in my chest and Margarida glanced over at me.

"Heavenly Father," I breathed, as she continues on, "What is she saying here? Is it possible that this is a direction we should consider? This is no small responsibility and we are a small group."

We had heard of course, on national news that children's gangs were so numerous and strong in some large cities that business people were hiring moonlighting policemen to shoot these street children. Jim had mentioned to me that our church needed to do something about it. Headlines in the morning newspapers often read like these:

"Street Children Found Shot on the Steps of the Cathedral Last Night."

"Street Children Considered Undesirable Are Being Executed."

That year, 1991, 306 children were killed in Rio de Janeiro and murdered in other large cities. Our church had seen the same problem on a smaller scale in our city but was at a loss to know what to do. We provided food baskets to the poor for an immediate relief with no social reform and no lasting help.

Was Dona Olga asking us to do something lasting?

She was a lady who took seriously the social needs of her community. "Would your church consider such a project? We have offered the idea to the two largest religious groups in the city. They said they didn't have program or personnel. "

She continued, "We have sent psychiatrists, medical people and educators to them and they have not been able to reach these children.

"Okay, let's talk. IF God is leading that way for our church, you cannot tie our hands on this aspect. The program would be to introduce each child to a personal relationship with Jesus Christ and a loving God. If they are going to say 'no' to drugs and crimes they must have inner strength. We would provide care for their physical, intellectual and emotional need, but true success will come with a spiritual change in their lives, " I said.

"Religion is a good path", she said.

"If Jesus is on that path, yes. He said 'I am the Way (path), the Truth, and the Life'."

"Give us three months to pray about this", I added. "During this time, we can prepare a program and draw together a support group. After this time, and with God's wisdom, we will try to come up with an answer."

What a difference that challenge was to make in our church, community and in my own life.

Making Plans

The church's committee members to consider the project were a factory owner, an industrialist, a policeman, an accountant, a retired school teacher, and missionaries Jim and Shirley Combs.

I called some Evangelical groups working with street children in other states of Brazil. Jim and I visited Homes in Minas Gerais, Sao Paulo ,Campinas, Ribeirao Preto, and Parana. They were so fine and helpful and shared copies of their constitution approved by their states and other documents and projects.

We listed some basic plans.

Accept children from birth to 12 years of age. House them seven days a week, 24 hours a day in a Christian family. A small group of 10 called 'casa lar" with a house mother.

All children of school age would attend public school with special tutoring done in the Home.

Volunteers. Professional volunteers such as psychologist, medical people, and educator had already shown interest. Dentists, doctors, nurses, therapists encouraged us with their offers to help. Hospitals and labs offered services at no charge. Vegetable vendors and merchants offered food. Educators offered to tutor the children.

Moral and religious training would be given on a daily basis in the home and through church attendance, camps, and retreats. Community pride and awareness would be taught. We would keep the children as long as necessary to give them an education and training in some profession.

We would teach the children to assume chores that would help them to reintegrate with the family and to be good citizens in their community.

To forgive their families and others who had mistreated them in the past.

To study, to serve others, to have good work ethics, to not lose hope. To pass forward their blessing's others.

One of the members said it would be like walking on water like Peter, but he voted with the others that, yes, the city needed a Christian home for street children, and, yes, our church could make a difference.

What's the Name?

We knew that there would be laws to register our Non-Governmental Organization and official registration of our information and name. Name?

The church members met and submitted possible names for the ministry of redeeming needy street children. After discussions they wanted a name in Portuguese. A name that would state the solution the Home wanted to address.

"Lar", meaning 'home' was preferred instead of "casa", meaning 'house'.

"Nova", meaning new chance to change their situation.

"Vida" meaning 'life'. Life in Christ, our hope.

So, the name became LAR NOVA VIDA.

While we were meeting and preparing a program, news got around and police cars started stopping in front of our house with children. Jim and I were living in a two-bedroom home with five people, but we made room for these children.

This year marks 31 years that we have cared for the needy children and families of our city, over 450 children. Little begging children didn't have to go to the streets because they could go to a Christian home.

Today some are now Christian adults who are evangelists, deacons, teachers, musicians, and parents. We have two who have studied law, two who have studied nursing, some are secretaries, factory workers, mechanics, sales persons, and apprentices in construction.

Some who went back to families with no structure, do not study, or work, or go to church. But the seed of the gospel and hope was planted in their hearts and we pray someone else will reach out a hand to love and help them.

Other cities asked us to place a house for children they needed to start under our name and administration. The cities would assume the finances and we could send Christians to direct the Home. At one time we had LNV homes in four cities with six houses. At one time we also had a LNV home for adult mentally challenged men. As cities regroup, their needs changed and some of these projects were closed, but we were able to leave a positive mark for Christ in their communities.

Since I have filled four books of the wonderful working of our Father God in the 30 years of Lar Nova Vida, I suggest you read these books. Get ready to be amazed and maybe shocked by stories of God-miracles. Stories about healings, power in the name of Jesus against evil spirits, God's provisions of food and protections. They can challenge your hearts, stir your souls, and show how God takes ordinary people to partner with Him to do extraordinary things!

One example of God supplying our need in a surprising way was when four of us from the USA arrived with offerings and a list. The government had not given the promised grant for five months to the Children's Home so items on our list to purchase were foods, appliances, furniture and more food. Also, we wanted to help pay some of their bills and host a party of hotdogs and ice cream in the park for the children and the workers and their children.

On the first day we arrived we saw their nine passengers Volks Van in a sad, sad shape. The door was wired shut to keep it from falling off in the street. The floors were rusty and wouldn't hold the bolts that fastened the benches that should stay up to hold the seat belts required to safely transport our children. SAD.

They needed another Van, of course, but how? They also needed food, and the gas and pharmacy bills do be paid. I would be leaving in three weeks. I knew that we needed it and wanted it, but we needed to put our knees to the floor and see what God thinks we need to do!

A friend thought he could find a Van in better shape for the equivalent of US$3,000 and maybe we could find enough people to raise that much.

In three weeks, we had raised most of the equivalent of three thousand American dollars, thanks to the help of Americans who came on the mission trip. But when the friend found a good Van in the third week, it was double the price.

Other Brazilians were consulted, and most of them said it was in excellent shape and was worth more than the asking price. The Lar Nova Vida budget was based on 'save before you buy.' Nothing on credit. A friend of the Children's Home heard about it and offered to loan us the second half. He said we could pay it back in payments as offerings came in.

There was nothing in the LNV budget to contribute. What the friend who offered the loan didn't know was that we had only a few small offerings from US Free Will Baptist. One church in Georgia, a couple in West Virginia, and three offerings in Oklahoma. It would take years to pay back US$3,000.

Oh, how I needed to talk to the Lord about this. He has faithfully supplied so that Brazilian Christians could shelter and plant seeds of hope in the lives of hundreds of children over the 30 years.

As I prayed and searched, a scripture from Psalms 62 came to mind. Is there something in there for us?

"My soul, wait silently for God alone. For my expectation is form Him. He only is my rock and my salvation; Trust in Him at all times, Pour out your heart before Him; God is a refuge for us."

Two of our mission team members had already left, and the day came for my daughter, Cindy, and me to catch our flight back to Oklahoma, and we still had not made a decision about the van. On the way to the airport, I kept meditation on the words, "wait silently for God alone" and then "my expectation is from Him" and "trust in Him at all times.'

Green light. Peace! A big silent YES came to me. "God alone." Okay, Lord, let's do it!

As soon as we checked in at the American Airlines counter, I asked Cindy to call the guys and tell them that the deal was a

GO. They soon put things in motion to close the deal the next day.

The night before we left, we saw one a teen from the Children's home baptized. That was what it was all about. They will have a safe vehicle. I left with a happy heart, ready to see how God was going to handle one more miracle.

We arrived at the OKC Will Rogers International Airport and then home safely. I wheeled my luggage into my bedroom and breathed, 'Home sweet home.' My son, Kemper, had put my three weeks of mail in the middle of my bed. I forgot about unpacking and started opening the pile of envelopes.

Many addresses I didn't even recognize. To my surprise, they held checks. Checks for Lar Nova Vida. I opened the ones with addresses I recognized. More checks. The dates were from before we were even debating and praying about a Van. God knew His plans, but the people didn't know the need when they decided to participate in the ministry.

Most of the prayer partners and sponsors of Lar Nova vida don't speak Portuguese or couldn't afford passports, visas, and airplane tickets to go visit the in Brazil. But they made it those days by obediently sending the offerings so God could work a miracle.

I punched in my phone calculator to add up the checks' values. Can you guess how much the total was? US$3,000! Yes, I was awed by God's foresight. His omniscience. He is my Father, and He loves needy little children and those who take care of them. He is a Father to the orphan and a husband to the widows, like me. I cried sitting on my bed and I have tears in my eyes now as I write.

Immediately I called Cindy to advise those in Brazil that we already had the money to pay off the loan. We had the amount necessary to pay off the loan before the Volks Van Kombi was delivered. Debt free. God and American friends partnered and supplied the need before the deal even came up.

It took a while to deliver, register, transfer documents, and complete all other paperwork needed for a vehicle to be donated to a non-profit organization. But the month before Christmas in summer-time Brazil in the main park in downtown Araras, Sao Paulo, before many witnesses, the keys and title of a beautiful white Volks Van Kombi were presented to the board and president of Lar Nova Vida. They did it up Brazilian style.

Across the one side of the Volks Van was stretched a banner.

(Translation)

"This Vehicle is an Offering of Love

In Memory of Missionary James Kemper Combs.

A memorial on the Altar of Jesus Christ."

What an adventure to put faith and trust in our Father God!

God Knew of Change Before We Did

At the time of this writing, we are redefining our role of rescuing needy children with Christian care in one of our cities. This month that city has taken away the grant they promised to us and have given it to another group that has no religious connections.

Our Children's Home is registered with the local, state, and federal governments as an ONG (Organization Non-Governmental) to shelter and care for children in small groups with a Christian environment. They gave a grant to spend on part of the salaries and in their zeal, perhaps, they felt they could put restrictions on how we care for the children, and who we arranged to care for them. They restricted volunteer help which cancelled our church groups who wanted to go for singing and devotions with the children. We could not insist they go to church and had to pay extra help to stay home with some while the others went to church. Well, you get the idea.

I realize that it will be old news by the time this book reaches your hands. But as young David remembered the bear and lion that God had already delivered into his hands before he faced the giant Goliath, we have 30 years of experience that God provided His great power and love in the past, and that helps us face this challenge. We ask God for wisdom, which He promises.

That is okay. God opened these homes and only He can close them. He has never failed us yet. We can already see how it actually frees us to return to our original plans in caring for our children without the restrictions of the government.

They city has a need for help to families with autistic children and a professional has asked us to consider it. We are studying the possibility of using professional volunteers and private backing to offer a project that uses adaptations of Music, Sports, Gardening, Games and Software, Scholastic tutoring, and Christian and psychological support for the family.

As I am writing this, I received notice that the project was approved! As I said, by the time this book reaches you, it may be old news but we know God is in control.

Family Highlights this term.

Other highlights of this term are that our daughter, Cindy, graduated at the Sao Luis College in Jaboticabal, with a Teacher's Degree, in 1991. Our son, Kemper, graduated from the University of Central Oklahoma with a degree in Business in 1992. We were 5,000 miles away on another continent and could not be there for our son's graduation. We are thankful for our relatives who made that trip to Oklahoma City to help in his celebration.

In 1993 we made a quick trip to Ribeiro Preto in the month of August for the birth of our first grandson, Jonathan Kemper (Combs) de Aquino. We were able to be with Cindy and the proud father, Jose Augusto, for that blessed day.

Jonathan is a fine Christian man, graduated with honors from Randall University in Oklahoma, and is married to a talented Christian young woman, Neveah. (Heaven spelled backwards.)

Our children were all born in Brazil and now our grandson was born in Brazil. Grand parenting is a blessing, right?

Chapter Twelve

Fifth State Side Assignment – 1994

My sister, Carolyn, and brother-in-law, George Aery, invited us to make their house our headquarters during our State Side Assignment. So, we moved to 16370 N. 52nd Avenue, Skiatook, Oklahoma. The city is 20 miles north and west of Tulsa, Oklahoma. Right now, it has a population of over 8,500. It was a good location for traveling and for other visiting relatives.

The Aery's were empty nesters and had a nice guest room where we could open our suitcases and relax when we were not traveling. They opened their home for family reunions that year we were there which helped us see more of the family.

George worked At Rockwell in Tulsa and Carolyn at State Farm Insurance in Skiatook, so we were by ourselves a lot. They were surrounded by beautiful trees and country roads and we enjoyed walking on pretty days. We were glad to help by preparing evening meals while they were working to show our gratitude, but the hours we spent sharing time together at home and in church were precious. There was a lot to catch up on after being gone for four years. And free rent helped our mission account, too!

When we did not have meetings marked for Wednesday nights, we attended the FWB church in Skiatook. Each time we sat by a young couple that had an infant son that I could hold.

It was a small group in a small town. Recently I was invited to speak at the church and that young man is now the pastor. Pastor Mitchell Leonard and wife Rachel.

The group wasn't small anymore, the church was full. The church members still love God, each other, reach out to their community, and have a passion to send the gospel around the world. The pastor honors the Word by wearing a tie, shares his pulpit with missionaries and other ministries for reports from those whom they support.

The worshipers also sing hymns projected on the wall. Quartets, trios, and solos prepare their messages in song. The children flow down the aisles collecting the 'penny march' in their little baskets for missions. My sister stopped by the bank each week to have a supply of coins to put into all their little baskets. Some things in the past are still working today to honor God. A refreshing experience.

Family Highlights

One highlight that year was an automobile accident in Kentucky on our way to the church parsonage where Ed and Nancy Cook ministered. We were about 15 miles from there. We were on Highway Route 60 after dark. Two cars facing us on the other side of the highway hit each other and one flew across the median and right toward us. Jim was driving.

I called out to him, "There is a car flying toward us!"

The lights came flying toward us and then the impact! It was sudden. It was shocking. Our car rolled over. Over into a ditch on the right side of the road and stopped right side up. My glasses were gone from my face and my watch was gone from my arm. My face and arms were full of small pieces of glass.

I looked over at Jim and he was in about the same shape.

He said, "I smell gasoline."

It seemed instantly that two young men came to our broken windows.

"Sir, we were following behind you and saw what happened. We are paramedics and we are going to help you get out of your car and an ambulance will take you to the hospital," one said.

"Oh, God sent you to be there at the right time. Thank you, "I said to the one at my window.

Jim said, "Don't let anyone come here smoking. I smell gasoline. I don't want this to catch on fire."

"Okay, sir. We will take care of that."

They carefully helped us out through the banged-up doors, anchored our necks in braces, put us on stretchers, and an ambulance took us to the hospital.

In the hospital, I kept asking about the young driver in the other car. They didn't have information yet or didn't want to share the information at that time. One said that maybe he had hurt his back. I prayed for him and thanked God we were alive.

Well, later we were told that the other young driver survived and said it wasn't his fault, and accepted no responsibility. The police report was that the two young drivers were racing at the red light and one clipped the other car and it came over the median into our car.

Jim gave someone information to call Pastor Ed Cook and Nancy, Jim's sister. I really don't know how long we stayed there before they came, but I seemed to be coming in and out of reality and it all ran together. God permitted us to be near their home when it all happened.

Nancy said that on her way she passed the place of the accident with all the lights flashing. One look at the wrecked car made her wonder how we even came out alive. We were in an old four door Lincoln without air bags, but we were both wearing seat belts. Later we saw the bruises from the belts across our chests which plus being in a heavy car probably saved our lives. Father God's hand was behind all of it. He wasn't finished with us yet.

We were finally taken to the parsonage of the West Wood (Free Will) Baptist) Church. The suit cases were sent with us and they were soggy messes. Smelling of gasoline. A total loss. Just like our car.

We salvaged some of the display we used in our presentation at churches when we reported about our last four years in Brazil. Also, salvaged were 100 yellow legal-size pages of a handwritten manuscript I had started after the requests of women from West Virginia, Kentucky and Oklahoma.

The Cooks were so good to take care of all the details and take care of us, too. They helped Jim with the details of taking our wrecked car somewhere. Nancy Gaye went to the wreck site and found Jim's broken glasses.

An optometrist from their church, Dr. Ron Pierce, quickly arranged for Jim another pair of glasses. God used several people those days.

Nancy Gaye even took off work a few days to take care of us. She helped Jim put on his socks and shoes and helped me get dressed. It seemed all the muscles in our bodies were wrenched.

I was scheduled to go to Brazil two days later so Nancy took me to the Charleston airport. She didn't think I should travel so soon so she arranged with the airlines to transport me in a wheelchair.

Jim perked up enough when Pastor Ed offered to take him to West Virginia to go deer hunting with his father and brothers. I believe they were there a week before Jim flew back to Oklahoma. Those Mountaineers had a great time after being apart for four years.

First Book, Second Chance

When we returned to Skiatook, we were checked out by the local chiropractor who became a friend. At the insurance office they estimated the cost of the total loss of the car, all of our belongings. I remember how helpful the State Farm agent was. She mentioned the amount allowed for 'pain and suffering'. Would we think the amount was fair?

Jim asked, "What do you mean 'pain and suffering'?"

She explained that it was customary and is included in all claims.

He said, "We are just glad to be alive. Pain and suffering are all part of the situation and I don't want anything for that."

She looked at him and shook her head, "Sir, you have just restored my faith in the human race."

Well, later he joked that if he had been in the USA a little longer before the accident, he may have accepted it!

With part of the insurance settlement, Jim bought me a laptop Notebook computer. He allowed me to leave him driving in silence as I typed for hours and hours over the thousands of miles, we traveled to meet our appointments in churches and schools from state to state. It was my first book about the Children's Home. The miracles that God performed to take care of the many needy children.

THEY DESERVE A SECOND CHANCE, was based on the stories we shared as we reported to our senders throughout the USA. The first 2,000 books sold out and it had to be reprinted later. That started my ministry of registering the marvelous provisions of God while we were in Brazil and then putting them in book form. For the books to go where I couldn't go. Four books are about transformation of lives in Brazil and one other book is about a man of God's battle to survive depression that led to suicide attempts while in our home.

Don Robirds was really encouraging me to write the first book in time to have it printed before we returned to Brazil. He and his wife Carol and children were on the airplane with us in 1964 as newly appointed missionaries. When our State Side Assignment was drawing closer to the end and our conference schedule increased, some professional friends helped me meet the deadline.

Larry Hampton from Oklahoma and Don's Editorial Assistant, Tammy Strickland, donated literally days of labor as we worked together in their offices in Antioch, Tennessee.

So, my first book was born in 1995 before we returned to Brazil. I had no idea that God would continue to 'write' more stories for me to witness and record.

Now, let me continue to put 80 years of my journey through the seasons of life on two continents and many addresses into one book. From birth to widowhood with glory adventures with God!

Chapter Thirteen

Sixth Term in Brazil - 1995

During this four-year term, we worked in two churches and *Lar Nova Vida* Children's Homes. It was a busy four years but one of the most rewarding.

The children's homes were growing each year. The city government offered to rent one house, but the court sent us more and more children. To maintain our mission to care for 10 children at a time with a Christian house mother, we continued to rent more houses. At one time we had three houses full.

Shelter for the Children

A safe shelter is a basic human need. We had sheltered over 90 children in seven different rented homes. Always dreaming and praying for our own roomy houses where we could better care for the children. We tried to wait upon the Lord, wait for His miracle. Well, God provided some miracles to help us build homes for our little ones.

One of the first things necessary was a plot of ground. We didn't have land! But that was no problem for God, who created this planet. Soon Senhor Carlos Alberto Fuganholi, a member of our free Will Baptist Church in Araras, felt impressed to donate land. After showing Jim several lots around town, he gave Jim his choice. Jim selected two lots in a semi-developed area because we needed to build two houses immediately.

Golden Shovel and the Surprise

Ours was the first to build in the Jardim Celina neighborhood, but first we had a ground breaking.

On ground breaking day, many friends and city officials gathered in the warm Brazilian sunshine on the donated lots surrounded by banners and balloons. We listened as our children sang in Portuguese, "The Wise Man Built His House Upon a Rock".

A new shovel had been painted gold, a big red ribbon tied around it, and the first shovelful of God's miracle was cut out. In the hole was placed a plastic box containing a Portuguese Bible, a floor plan, and a photo of the children and a little printed program of the day's event.

We had a surprise coming. Jim gave a short history of the ministry and commented that we had US$5,000, thanks to a Youth Group from Oklahoma. A ripple of laughter ran through the crowd. What we saw as a wonderful beginning looked very weak to the general public in light of the $250,000 project we had just presented.

The city mayor, Senhor Pedro Eliseu, asked to say a few words. He expressed his appreciation for the ministry of our church, which had helped his son who was attending there and for the contribution of Lar Nova Vida to the community.

Then came the surprise. He admired our willingness to begin construction with so little money but he offered a gift from community funds – $50,000. He kept his word. Ten months of

$5,000 per month was a great boost to help with labor costs. Enough to start the foundation.

In my other books you can enjoy reading in greater details about the miracles God provided. The city sent numerous truckloads of dirt. Community friends donated hundreds of sacks of cement and tons of gravel, rock, and sand. Others donated wood, electrical and plumbing material. And lots and lots of bricks.

Nestle Company donated windows and doors. One day trucks arrived with twelve tons of floor tile. Another group donated money for labor for placing stucco on 4,000 square feet of walls. Rotary Club donated a commercial kitchen for the cafeteria.

Along with the two houses for the children and house parents, the project included a large cafeteria, a laundry room, offices, an infirmary, and two workshops. Except for the seed money donated by Oklahoma youth, our miracle buildings had been erected with money and material donated from Brazilian people, thankful to have a solution for the growing population of street children. It was truly a house that LOVE built.

Grand Dedication

Among the noise and festivities of that glorious March day, we had the dedication of the new homes of *Lar Nova Vida*. The present and former mayors were invited, representatives of the courts and merchants, school official and pastors were invited.

Several politicians were present in an unusual meeting of different political party leaders. They were on neutral ground, so it was a fraternal, historical celebration of something good for their city.

The children's choir sang for the crowd and I was so proud of them. Several adults listened with tears in their eyes. Including mine.

Dr. Mark Brashier, from my home church of Rejoice FWB church in Owasso, represented the youth who sent the first offering, and Jim interpreted for him. Ex-mayor, Pedro Eliseu, and present mayor, Warley Colombini, and vice-mayor, Carleto Denardi, all spoke.

Also present were a congressman, Dr. Nelson Salome, the Secretary of Education, Secretary of Health, Secretary of Social Welfare, the Governor of the Rotary club, local pastors and Christian friends.   They all added their prayers and encouragement.

After an exhausting and exhilarating day, we thanked God. "He is able to do exceedingly abundantly above all that we ask or think, according to the power that works in us."

Jardim Candida Church

The mother church downtown considered planting five churches throughout the city of Araras. On the east side of the main Anhanquera Highway, there was no evangelical church. A couple living on that side opened their small front porch for home Bible study groups. Sr. Joaquim and Dona Julia. The group grew, so a larger place was rented. It kept growing so land was purchased and a permanent building was planned. Jim sketched the design and with the help of an architect/engineer friend, plans were drawn and presented to the authorities.

The mother church downtown had called a Brazilian pastor and he sent the children from Lar Nova Vida to the new group. That gave us a great group of children and youth to make our work there more complete.

The neighborhood now had a Bible preaching church where lives were transformed and baptized. Couples were married and babies were dedicated. Believers were discipled and the lives of the deceased were celebrated.

Missionary Conferences, Vacation Bible School, neighborhood street events, special holiday cantatas, and youth programs helped the new church grow spiritually.

Jardim Maraba' Church

Years before we had started a weekly meeting at a sugar plantation where the family of Senhor Jose Mendes and his many children accepted Christ. Three of their sons, Oripes, Joaquim, and Joao, hitch hiked rides to our small rented building about a block from our house on *Rua Tiradentes.*

By the time that our church bought land and built their building on *Rua 24 de Marco*, Sr. Joaquim and family had moved from the plantation to a small house on the other side of town. Jim, together with the church, studied the need to start a preaching point there. Sr. Joaquim's house was very small but the group enjoyed meeting in his back yard. (He also had a machine there to make *garapa from* sugar cane juice which the group enjoyed.)

We bought a piece of land on the corner of *Espirito Santo* Street in front of the *Praca da Biblia.* Before the Sunday School rooms were built in the back, we had Bible lessons for the children in the park in front of the church.

During the first years, Sr. Joaquim and other laymen led the Bible studies and preaching. Sr. Joaquim and sons played the instruments and led in praise music. Jim and I trained and provided material behind the scenes and the group grew at one time larger than the mother church.

The church opened its arms to the community and offered Literacy Classes to adults using a method based on the Bible. Sugar Plantations bussed in students and a national magazine recorded that it grew to be the largest literacy school in all Brazil.

Their vision included supporting missions with prayer and offerings. For many years for some reason, it remained a mission and preaching point after we left the area.

But today it is a vibrant organized church led by Pastor Jose Assuncao and wife Leslie. Their sons and the family of Afonso and Maria Araujo have been faithful workers for many years.

Family Highlights That Term

While we were in Brazil, our youngest daughter, Tania Marita, graduated with honors from Oklahoma Central University in OKC with a degree in business in 1996.

She returned to our home in Brazil and in 1998 married a young man from Ribeirao Preto, Rodrigo Feirreira. They grew up together at youth camps and in church where his father was a deacon. He was a young widower with a five-year-old son,

Daniel. When Rodrigo started riding his motorcycle for over two hours to date our daughter, we realized that she had chosen him as "the one".

They were married at the *Igreja Batista Livre* where her sister had married. Once again friends from the many addresses where we had lived filled the church and stayed for the wedding feast.

At the back of our property, we had decorated a covered shelter and filled it with folding tables and chairs and placed floating lit candles in the swimming pool. A special table was beautifully prepared for the wedding cake.

Jim prepared '*churrasco*" meat to grill for 300 people. He had friends to help him grill, I had Cindy and others to help serve the rice and vinaigrette, Kemper and Marco Antonio helped with the Guarana' soft drinks. We celebrated into the night and we gained a wonderful, talented new son and a beautiful little grandson.

More Brazilian Born Grandchildren

During that term we took a road trip to be present for the birth of our first granddaughter in August of 1995. Julia de Aquino. She had big blue eyes and wavy hair like her mother. One of her trips as a child to the USA, she played children's soccer and surprised her coach.

He asked, "Who is that tiny little girl who is our terrific goalie today?"

Someone explained, "She just moved to Oklahoma and played with her brothers in Brazil."

Brazil was the only country who had won the World Soccer Cups five times, so that seemed to be enough of any answer for the coach.

Julia is now a graduate with honors from Randall University in Moore, Oklahoma. She sings, plays her guitar and composes music from her sensitive heart. She is my go-to technician when I produce these books on my old computer.

We took that same trip in 1998 to Ribeirao Preto for the birth of our grandson David William de Aquino. He had darker hair and really favored his father, Jose Augusto. He grew up as a talented athlete and kept us entertained with his fun for life. He is now an insurance agent and I just saw a video of his first sermon.

Chapter Fourteen

Sixth State Side Assignment - 1999

For this State-Side Assignment we had the blessing to move in with my parents at 301 N. Atlanta in Owasso, Oklahoma. Only later did we find out how important that move was. My father was almost 90 and mother was four years younger.

We had a great time being together in their home in the city where I went to school and where he started the Free Will Baptist Church. We could use their home as headquarters while we visited the churches nearby and then visit with my parents in all of our free time. They had been so supportive emotionally and spiritually. That helped us get to Brazil and to stay in Brazil all those years apart. But they supported us financially when they could.

My father had had a knee surgery that left him without being able to straighten his leg. He had a low grade of fever for two years. His doctor did not give a solution for his problem so he was in a wheelchair. Family members checked in on them from time to time.

Mother and Heart Problems

Mother started having heart trouble and then strokes. I was glad I could be there to help. She would stay awake at night emptying her chest of drawers and then refolding and placing everything again neatly in the drawers. Father would call to be at night and ask me to get up and help her get back to bed. I just went to her room and sat with her a while and let her talk. Finally, she would want to get in bed.

One day Mother had another very serious heart attack and was taken to the hospital. My four sisters and I divided our time between helping our Father at home and our Mother in the hospital. My mother was over the crisis and it was my turn in the hospital. Talking with her doctor about her care, I offered that we would get a nurse and adapt the home for her care.

He said, NO! I didn't know doctors had that much authority in those matters. He said he would not release her from the hospital until we had her enrolled in a rehab home.

I went home and discussed it with my father and four sisters. They got her enrolled in a Baptist Care Center about two miles from their home. The home was fully equipped with personnel trained to help, but my sisters and I took two-day turns in staying with mother during the day. It was hard on Father and he wanted to see her every day.

Father Changes Addresses

One night Jim and I went to a missionary service at a church nearby and left Father at home. When we returned home that night, we discovered that Father was taken to the hospital. He said he went to lock the back door but didn't lock his wheelchair, so when he leaned toward the door the chair rolled and he fell and broke his leg. He dragged himself to a phone and called my sister and she sent an ambulance that took him to the hospital.

Mother had more strokes and could not sit up, eat by herself, or talk except straining to stutter 'TaTaTa.' When we told Mother about his accident, she seemed to beg to go to the hospital to see him. We told her to wait until he came home and he would go by to see her. He never did.

His vital signs were great and he was in good spirits. Some pastors visited him in the hospital and he led in prayer. When I went to see him, the nurses said he had told them about my being a missionary to Brazil and other family history. He made friends easily and was to leave the hospital soon.

Then suddenly something went wrong. I went to the hospital to visit him and saw something wasn't right. It was learned the hospital had accidently given him medicine he was allergic to and his body was reacting violently and started to shut down. Soon he was in no pain. God had transported him to his new address in heaven. Spring, 2000.

The family asked me to speak the Eulogy of our dear father and Bro. Leonard Pirtle to speak at the celebration of his life. There was a choir of preachers on the stage of Rejoice FWB church that led us in "How Great Thou Art." My mother was pushed in her wheel chair up to the casket and they lifted her up in her chair so she could kiss his cold skin.

Mother was not able to speak where we could understand. She liked to watch the Gaither Family Music Concerts on tape we arranged in her room. He eyes would light up and she would tap her fingers on her sheets. But an amazing thing happened when we five girls gathered around her bed and sang. She would sing words and harmonize in alto. Some of the nurses had never heard her speak and were so surprised. Deep in our souls is music and hers came out as a gift to us. Glory!

To Wait or Not to Wait

I was struggling with the date for our return to Brazil and I needed to hear from the Lord and receive a 'hug' from Him.

We had been away from Brazil for almost a year, and we yearned to get back to our people, the children and ministry. About returning we had peace.

Our father had been the healthier of the two, but passed away one month before. Mother had been in the Baptist Care Center now for four months and my sisters went daily to the center to feed her meals and to do what they could. I helped out when we weren't on the road in services. This is the mother who instilled the love for missions in my heart and had sacrificially been separated from us since 1964 and from her grandchildren and great grandchildren who were born in Brazil.

I was torn between two important responsibilities. Should I wait awhile before leaving? I want to do my share of helping. If I wait, for how long?

One Tuesday morning, about 7:45 a. m., two weeks before we were to return to Brazil, I was in the Baptist Care Center on my way to feed breakfast to my mother.

As I passed the waiting room and looked at the magazine rack a thought came, "Pick up the hymnal." Usually there were no hymnals there but when I went over to the rack, there was a red one on the bottom shelf.

When I returned to her room, I waited for a free moment, read my Proverb for the morning, and reached for the hymnal. It fell opened to the song entitled, "Here is My Life." It was not a hymnal I had used, and I did not know the tune but part of the words was these:

"Lord, I give my life to you,

My TIME, my talents, each day new.

With faith to witness to your plan,

With hope to gladly take my stand.

And love to minister to man.

I cannot WAIT. I cannot WAIT!

Here is my life, I want to live it.

Here is my life, I want to give it.

Serving my fellowman, doing The Will of God."

My dear mother could not express herself as I looked at her in that hospital bed through teary eyes. But I remembered her words when asked by other women how she could give up her children and grandchildren to live so far away.

She answered, "I would rather my children be in God's will wherever He leads, than to have them live next door out of His will."

The poem had been around since Ed Seabough wrote it in 1969 and was saved for me for that moment.

A hymnal out of place. An answer sought. An answer given by the voice of my Lord with a gentle 'hug'.

Chapter Fifteen

Seventh Term In Brazil –2000

The Children's Homes seemed to be going well. The three churches had Brazilian pastors, in their own buildings, and the Children Home was in its new houses and was under Brazilian leadership.

We had a wonderful year of receiving mission groups to visit us from USA churches, E-Teams, College Teams, and our friends. At first, we housed them with Brazilian Christians, in the church and in our home. Then we closed in our open shed at the back of our property to make our "Hospitality House'. It had bunk beds for 12 people, kitchen and four bathrooms.

We also had sleep overs for our Lar Nova Vida children. Our swimming pool was used for baptism and once a month we invited the three FWB churches and the *Lar Nova Vida* families for a covered dish lunch. What a blessing it was to have that fellowship time.

Family Highlights

In 2001 I made a quick trip to Oklahoma for the birth of another granddaughter, Bianca Ferreira. Tania and Rodrigo's baby girl. So beautiful and so much hair! She was registered with both Consulates and has dual citizenship just like my other grandchildren.

She is a good student, learned to play instruments in band and in church, played Volley Ball in High school, sang the National

Anthem at one of her games, and is now a student at Randall University. That is where she met her husband, Jacob Partridge, and they are working at Summit FWB church where Pastor Mitch Wagner and wife Taryn are. At this moment they are in Sugar Land, Texas, interning for the summer at Eagle Heights FWB Church, where Pastor Randy Puckett and wife Shelly minister.

Staying Busy Training Others

A missionary arrives in an area to work himself out of a job. A little different from a pastor's agenda. We train the national people to eventually take over. Then we move on to a new work in that town or possibly in another city suggested by the Field Council of missionaries.

Jim was invited to preach at the churches in town and served as a mentor to the leaders. I was invited to conduct seminary for women's groups and to help leaders prepare materials. I assisted in mentoring the staff at the Children Homes. We were careful to keep a low profile and help behind the scenes. But we were busier than ever!

However, after a while, my husband and partner in ministry seemed restless. Was it the fall of the currency exchange? Were the ministries in good hands? Or that our Brazilian-born children and grandchildren were 5,000 miles away with us?

He couldn't tell me.

A Short Trip to the USA - 2004

We arrived in Brazil in 1964 and Jim wanted to retire from International Missions Of Free Will Baptist in 2004. We made a quick trip to talk to our IM department tin Tennessee about our plans. They asked us to continue on the field. We thanked our supporters and advised our families that we would be returning someday. After four months we returned to Brazil.

Back to Brazil for Four More Years.

We continued to live in Brazil for four more years and continued in all our ministries the same as before (except with no salary, ha) and it was a good fruitful time.

Pastor Leonard Pirtle reminded me that there is a season for everything. If God gave us a green light to return to the USA, then doors would open for ministry with our family and among Christian ministries in the United States. I kept these things in my heart.

Family Highlights

Papaw Combs Changed His Address to Heaven

We had not been back to Brazil very long when the Combs family called us in 2003 that Rev. Cecil, Papaw Combs, was very sick. Jim caught a plane to Oklahoma and rode with his sister, Judy, from Oklahoma to be with their father and help his siblings during his father's last days.

After a time, he returned to Oklahoma and then to Brazil. Jim's sisters and brothers from North Carolina, Oklahoma, and West Virginia continued to faithfully and lovingly help Dad Combs. He was a man who was a leader in the states where he pastored – West Virginia, Georgia, and Florida. He was loved and admired. He was a pastor, master builder, state denominational leader, a Certified Public Accountant and loving husband. He fathered 15 children, grandfather to 37, great grandfather to 58, and great-great- grandfather to three children.

In November the family called again saying that he lost his battle with cancer but was completely healed in heaven. Since Jim had been with him shortly before he moved to his heavenly address, he chose not to go to the funeral in West Virginia. It was bitter-sweet news being so far away, but our grandchildren were there.

Baby Isabela

Once again, I flew to Oklahoma for the birth of our granddaughter, Isabela Ferreira, in 2005. Tania and Rodrigo's child. She was full of energy and rhythm and loved to be heard and seen.

She played sports in school and in private church gymnasiums. She sang in the school choirs and sang the National Anthem at one of their ball games and plays the ukulele.

Isabela was the youngest granddaughter when we arrived and we had many sleep overs with her. She was the last to sit on her grandfather's lap while she twisted him around her little finger. She is a genuine dog lover. She was registered at both Embassies and has dual citizenship as our other grandchildren have.

She was the youngest and asked the most questions.

"Grandma, when was the first time someone called you a 'widow'?"

"Grandma, do you ever take off Grandpa's wedding ring?"

"Grandma, would you rather be with Grandpa in heaven or here with us?"

God had given us a green light to come to Oklahoma to be with our children, to live life with them. I could tell her that at her young age. I told her I wanted to see her graduate from high school, fall in love with a man God chooses, make me a Bis-avo' (great grandmother). It looks like I may see her graduate in less than a year at this writing.

Today she helps in the church nursery and is a quieter, lovely young lady.

Another Wedding in Brazil

In 2005 our son, Kemper Jonathan, married a young lady from the church. The wedding was at our newest church in town in Jardim Candida. In Brazil a church wedding is not recognized by the government so you must also get married at the Justice of the Peace. Kemper invited a pastor friend from Campinas who was also a Justice of the Peace. It was beautiful and Kemper sang to his beautiful bride. He said it was the happiest day of his life.

Instead of the *churrasco* wedding feast like his sisters had, he suggested to invite the wedding party of about 300 *to Pizzaria Castellano* for *rodizio* style service. His father was surprised but it made it much easier for him. Even the restaurant owner said they had never had a wedding party in their place.

Rodizio pizza is served by waiters of about 15 different types of pizzas. As they pass by your table you shake your head yes or no and wait for the next one served. They end up the night with desert choices like white and brown chocolate drizzled on different fruits...on pizzas. They did have a wedding cake and Guarana'.

The Gringos were good sports and tried some that had greens, and vegetables, eggs, sardines, tuna, and other combinations that they had never seen. Not every Brazilian pizza has cheese or tomato sauce.

They were a mission group from my home church in Owasso, Oklahoma visiting us, Rejoice FWB Church. They helped make the *genuflexorio* (kneeling bench) that was used in the wedding ceremony. They gave disposable photo cameras to each table at the restaurant and people took great candid shots and gave them to the groom to have developed. The *Gringos* added a lot to the wedding feast and it was a blast to see so many people trying to communicate not knowing the other's language.

Mother Roberts Moved Her Address

My family called that Mother seemed to be ready to move her address to heaven and asked if I could try to get home before she passed to visit with them at the Baptist Home. I immediately arranged a plane ticket from Sao Paulo Airport to the Tulsa International Airport on the Saturday night before Easter in 2006. It was an all-night flight and I arrived the next morning. My sister Carolyn and her husband George met me. They hugged me and were a little quiet so I guessed they were waiting for me to ask.

The night I was traveling, Mother's grandchildren, children, her only living sister, Wanda Muse, and others were there singing with guitar music. One of the girls told her that everyone was okay and she didn't need to hold on any longer. If Jesus was calling, she should feel free to go on with the angels to take her to heaven to meet her Savior, husband, her son, parents and so many more. We would all meet again someday.

She closed her eyes and left this planet earth completely healed!

I stayed for the Celebration of her beautiful life and once again the family asked me to give the eulogy. So many others were there at Rejoice FWB Church with Bro. Leonard Pirtle officiating. Many who were former church members who had been touched by this precious servant of God were present.

Green light!

God seemed to say he was opening the way to return 'home'. Transformation! A change came over Jim. He loved the Brazilian people as much as I. He was great in the language. But a change came over him. While my heart was heavy and hurting at the thought of all we were leaving and I seemed to be stuck on the caution light, his heart was light just planning on what we could be facing by God's guidance.

And Jim was right. Our children and family were happy. The Brazilian leadership was shocked and sad, but wanted God's will, also. We were more intense in training and encouraging them for all that God had for them.

We put our home up for sale. Jim thought it better to sell the furniture, kitchen supplies, towels and linens, décor and paintings hanging on the wall and just walk away. For the flight home we could only take two suitcases each. How to put 44 years in two suitcases? I am a list maker and I had many lists to cover for us to catch that plane

Photos Of My SUMMER SEASON - USA

Nashville, Tennessee – 1960 – Free Will Baptist Bible College (now Welch College)

Six Roommates in Bunk Beds

RICHLAND HALL

PRESIDENT

TREASURER

Photos Of My SUMMER SEASON - Brazil

Leaving for Brazil – 1964   Miami, Fla

Church Building site -Araras, SP -1967

Missionaries in Brazil

Our FWB Churches In Araras, Sao Paulo

(First) Igreja Batista Livre de Araras, Sao Paulo

Segunda (Second) Igreja Batista Livre, Araras,SP

Terceira (Third) Igreja Batista Livre, Araras, SP

Visiting in the Amazon Jungle, Territorio de Roraima

Indians in Amazon Jungle meeting us at the plane. Woops!

At the top of the Mountain.

Nurse, Linguist, Teacher

At the Trading Post for Work on the Airstrip

Three Brazilian Free Will Baptist Jungle Pilots

Junior T.- Jose P.- Tania - Lelis F –Cindy –Kemper –Shirley –Jim C.

Not Pictured, most recent – Jefferson Gaino, Pilot

Our young Family

Church Started on their Front Porch

Sra. Julia   Sr. Joaquim

Many Baptism in Araras, Sao Paulo

Baptism in the Tubarao River Before the Flood

. Tubarao River After the Flood

Church Group After the Tubarao River Flood

Tubarao Group at Camp in Uruguary. Becky Robinson
leading.

In Front of the House-Tubarao, S.C.

Neighbors – The Lavnio Thizon family attended the church

Photos Of My SUMMER SEASON – USA

After the Tubarao Flood

Shirley Graduates –American Christian College

"Mom And Dad' Dedicated To The Cause

American Christian C olldege

Our family in their Yearbook

Serving students while waiting for the rebuilding of *Tubarao*, Santa Catarina, before returning to Brazil. American Christian College, Tulsa, Oklahoma

Jose Mendes   Jim C.   Joao Barbosa

Men who Helped Open Maraba' Church

Women's Meeting at My Chacara House

Women's Meeting at the Church

My Summer Season - Araras

Bride Cindy   Bride Tania   Groom Kemper

First House – Alto das Araras

Second House – Chacara Morado do Sol

Jesse'   Susana   Marco A.   Ana C.   Claudiana
Victori

Brazilian Foster Son and Family (On his birthday)

My Summer Season – Brazil – Lar Nova Vida

Finally a Permanent Home – Jd. Celina, Araras

1999   Donated Tricycles

Lar Nova Vida Family at Jd. Candida FWB Chirch

LNV Children's Choir

Laar Nova Vida – Youth Orquestr

Some Partners Who caught the Vision of **Rescuing Children**

True Family Siblings- Ok.

Siblings – Janice and Janet-Ok

Dr. Jim and Bobbie Jo Lee -Georgia
Pam Wilson - Kansas
(Marcelo and   Dra. Marina)-- Jiu-Jitsu Project

Brad & Deb Bickerstaff-Ok.   Bobbie Jean - Florida
No photo: Jim and Karen Circle, W.V.,
Dibble FWB Church, Ok.
Iron Chapel FWB Church, Ok. , & Others! Thanks.

Missions Conferences Hillsdale/Randall University
Introducing Students, Faculty, andf Staff to Our Missionaries
While serving there – 1980-1984

Cousineous,I.C. –Bryans,-I.C. –Sparks,Spain -Allen, I.C. –
Archer, Ok.

Laura Bell Barnard, pioneer –India

-      Shirley combs - Brazil

Teague, France - Bishop, Japan

<u>Other Participants. No photos:</u> Archie Mayhew ,I. C. Africa

Earnie Deeds, Brazil – Judy Smith, Japan – J. Smith, Weathrford

Jerry Banks, Japan – Eddie Payne, I.C. – Paul Thompson, Arizona

Talent, France -Fulcher, Hispanics USA –Callaway, Spain- Dickens, I.C.

Paul Robinson, Uruguay

John & Kay Metcalf, Appointees

Died in Car Crash Before Reaching Brazil

Kednnedy, Calif –Bishop, Japan – Lee, I.C. –Arnold, C. Amer

-Bishop, Japan-Filkin, I.C.

"Jesus loves the Little Children of the World "

"Jesus loves the Little Children of the World "

Part Three

My Autumn Season
2008-2017

"Therefore, we do not lose heart,
Even though our outward man is perishing,
Yet the inward man is being
Renewed day by day."
2 Corinthians 4

Chapter Sixteen

AUTUMN SEASON BEGINS

A Change Of Continents –Nov., 2008

Everything we left there in Brazil, God has given us again and more. We are blessed.

This adventure was too big for me, so I didn't even make a list this time. For re-entry into the USA, we had very little to start with. The Word says that God is able to do exceedingly abundantly above all that I could ask or think, so why not just let Him make the lists from now on.

God's List

We arrived the day after Thanksgiving in 2008 to spend the holiday with our children and grandchildren. God's list had already started, and He had more surprises for us.

Transportation -Our niece, Lancia, already had a Van waiting for us at a very low price. Check mark for God's list. Yes!

Housing – We went to the bank, but since we had not lived in the USA for many years, we had no credit. We pay cash for everything, which I thought was good. Loan rejected.

We put a bid on a HUD (repossessed) house but they did not encourage us since our down payment was very small.

A few days later the bank called and said our loan was approved after all. Check mark for God's list. Yes!

Two hours later HUD housing called that even though our down payment was lower than others, our bid was approved. Check mark for God's list. Yes!

Finally, after spending a lot to repair the house, we had a USA address, and a home. But empty.

Empty house – Friends and family, and yard sales were great to help us find the essentials to put in our home. Beds, sofas, tables and chairs, and even clothes in the closet.

The missionary Provision Closet from International Missions in Tennessee, opened its doors for retiring missionaries and we loaded our Van with all those wonderful gifts. Pots and pans, sheets and towels, and even wall décor.

Sound familiar? Those were the very things we turned our backs on when we left Brazil. Check mark for God's list. Yes.

Culture Shock Re-entry

God still had more on His list. We left behind a lifetime of friends and family and 44 years of a different language, different food and climate. Now once again we could talk, sing, worship, and laugh in our own native tongue – English.

Well, except for strange expressions: bff, brb, ty, ttyl, yw, thx and lol. (I thought that lol meant lots of love.) LOL!! The difference between Tweet and Twitter? Siris and Google? The difference between Messages, Messenger, and WhatsApp.

At the market that asked things like 'Paper or Plastic'? Uh I'm sorry, but can you repeat that, please? If you have never shopped with a debit card, questions like 'slide? Chip? Cash return? Punch yellow or green?

You have to admit that you have never deposited a check at a drive-through. You have never used a self-serve gas pump. Never driven your car through a drive-through car wash. You have to punch "no, no, no" buttons just to get a simple car wash.

Where are the clothes lines?

You notice how often folks go to fast-foods and restaurants to eat. How can it be cheaper to order it readymade than buy material to make it at home?

Good adjustments

Good adjustments –I was so ready for hot water in all the sinks, clothes dryers, heat and air everywhere, even in the stores and churches. So good.

Since our cars in Brazil were always standard shift, it was nice to go to an automatic car, and learn to use cruise control. Nice!

I learned to edit and send photos right from my phone. I can send texts to family instead of bothering them at work. Amazing.

Preparing a meal is so much easier, faster and convenient here. It seems less trouble than going out to eat and standing in line. Satisfying.

Empty Agendas – Bench warmers?

We chose a FWB church where some of our children were attending. Kingsview church. We fell in love with the people and their vision as a church. At first, we enjoyed just sitting on the church bench and worshipping together in our own native language. Waiting to see how God wanted us to serve.

We didn't need to write, translate, and print off material for the church leaders to use. We didn't need to transport families to their homes because the buses didn't run after evening church services ended. So, we enjoyed the church bench – for a while.

Full Agenda – Family

One of the new assignments we felt God sent us here to do was to live life with our children and grandchildren. Our opportunities were at their sports events, music concerts, class plays, Grandparent's Days, birthdays, and graduations. And family meals.

Family reunions with my Roberts family in Oklahoma, four living siblings plus their families, was a blessing. Since Jim had ten living siblings scattered throughout the USA, we enjoyed the Combs Reunions, usually meeting in Wild, Wonderful, West Virginia.

We had a lot of catching up to do.

During this time, I was asked to present two more family eulogies. In my home in Moore, I held a celebration of our oldest sister's, Dean Hale, eightieth birthday. We had fun reminding her of her journey with us from the list I had made. Then, I was asked to give her eulogy at her funeral after her sudden home-going. Once again, we celebrated her life but with her new move to heaven. Pastor Leonard Pirtle was there again to comfort our hearts from the promises of the Word.

We celebrated our next sister, Alene, at a birthday party given for her by my sister, Dolores. After her battle with cancer treatments and surgeries, we gathered together again, another eulogy, to celebrate her home-going. Whether it was for a wedding or a funeral, our family many times called Pastor Leonard Pirtle, to be with us. He again led the celebration of the life of one more member of the Roberts family.

It was easier to grieve with family when we lived in the same country together. One of Jim's brother, Bob, and his wife, Charlotte, and one of Jim's sisters, Mary Ruth, also moved their addresses to heaven. And it is easier to grieve when we know they are there in heaven, completely healed.

Our journey to HOME gets sweeter.

Full Agenda – Ministry

A new friend in our Sunday School class, Pat Fish, invited Jim and me to sing in the Community Joy Choir of about 25 people from several churches. There were six members from our church who were participating. We visited each Thursday a different hospital, or memory care homes, and assisted living centers to sing and love on the elderly, handicapped, and their caregivers.

Our Sunday School class teacher, Earnie Deeds, was the president of a monthly meeting named OASIS (Older Adults Still in Service). Jim and I joined and fellowshipped with retired lay people, preachers, deacons, and their spouses.

At Kingsview Church, Jim and I volunteered for the nursery. I enjoyed helping in Vacation Bible School and teaching the three- to five-year-olds in Sunday School with my friend Pat.

We formed a WAC (Women Active for Christ) day meeting for missionary minded prayer warriors. Jim received opportunities to preach in various churches, and for a year and a half he was interim pastor and preached three times a week.

A highlight for us was that a couple from Albany, Georgia. Dr. Jim and Bobbie Jo Lee, blessed us with tickets to return to our beloved Brazil to serve for a month or so each year.

God's list was more than we could imagine and it was amazing. What he had on the list next introduced me to my New Normal.

Photos of My Autumn Season – USA

Jim and Shirley Combs

Tania   Shirley   Kemper   Jim   Cindy

Combs Family - Moore

Grandchildren – Moore, Ok

Front Row: Bela, Shirley, Nevaeh, Jonathan, Julia

Back Row: Daniel, Bianca, Jacob, David

Jonathan & Nevaeh de Aquino

Jacob & Bianca (Ferreira) Partridge

Great Grandson Leon & Daniel

My Autumn Season – Brazil

Friends Meeting Us on One of our Trips Back.

We Hosted **Many E-Teams, and Mission Groups**

30th Anniversary of Lar Nova Vida Childdren's Homes Ex-residents Choir

Part Four

My Winter Season
2017- 20??

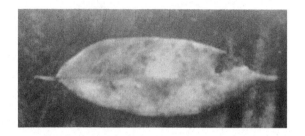

"Now also when I am old and grayheaded,

O God, do not forsake me,

Until I declare Your strength

to this generation,

Your power to everyone who is to come. "

Psalms71:18

Chapter Seventeen

Winter Season Begins- 2017

Widowhood and New Normal

Two days after Thanksgiving 2016 at our daughter Cindy's house, Jim went to his VA doctor on a Saturday morning with a tummy ache. I offered to go with him, but he told me to go on to work at Wood Creations showroom, and he would call later. My work would be close to the VA hospital in Oklahoma City. So, I went to work not knowing what a heart-breaking day that would be.

By the afternoon with no word from him, I called his cell number. He answered, "Well, honey, I have been taking tests for hours."

I asked, "What are they finding?"

Then came the answer we were not prepared for. "They say I have stage four cancer, and I have three to four months to live."

Our son-in-law, Rodrigo, passed by my counter at that moment.

After I told him he said, "Go right now to the hospital, and I will close up and be there soon."

I guess Rodrigo called our other children because soon we all surrounded the bed of the man who had always been healthy and happy. We had recently traveled to Brazil. He was helping handicapped students on and off their special school bus. So full of life and plans. Our bucket list had a hole in it.

God had another travel plan for Jimmy Kemper Combs just two months later. We had shared 23 addresses together for almost 54 years when God changed Jim's to a new address. A move I couldn't make with him. Family was in the living room, and I was on the bed with him holding his hand. I watched him take his last breath before I called the others to his bedside.

We celebrated his life on February 11, at Randall University in Oklahoma, with about 500 family and friends present, but still in a little shock at the suddenness of it all.

The Last Appointments

But Jim taught us how to look at death with his songs, silly jokes, and funeral plans. At the hospital he joked with the doctors and nurses and they commented at his unusual attitude. After the young doctors and nurses surrounding his bed told him of his diagnosis. Advanced cancer. No treatment. Three to four months to live. So sorry.

He said, "I need a doctor."

The young group looked at each other and one said, "Of, course, Mr. Combs, if you want another doctor's opinion…"

Jim interrupted, "I need a Dr. Pepper."

That broke the serious moment and one replied,

"Sir, you can have all the Dr. Pepper you want to drink."

Our grandchildren were there and Jonathan stood up immediately and left. He returned with a two-liter bottle of just what the "doctor ordered."

One day a nurse was in his hospital room and we were talking together. Jim turned from his side on to his back and said to me, "Just think, I'll never have to mow the grass or cut my toenails again."

The nurse had an answer, "You know, don't you, that your toenails continue to grow while you are in the casket."

He smiled, "You know what one casket said to the other casket? "

The kids shook their heads, no.

"Uh, is that you coffin?" (coughing)

He kept us entertained, but tears escaped from the grandchildren's eyes. It was still difficult on the young.

During the last days of his life, he was helped up the steps of the stage of Randall University and then he sat in a chair and took the microphone. Dr. Mark Brashier had asked Jim to speak to the students about living and dying. He talked seriously with them and then sang a little and told some jokes.

On Sunday morning he preached sitting in a chair at Iron chapel FWB church, and on Sunday evening he spoke at Dibble FWB Church. He participated there in his last Lord's Supper and feet washing service. He went with me one more time to sing with the Community Joy Choir in an assisted living facility, seated as he sang.

He soon spent more days in his recliner and in bed planning his funeral. His spiritual children and co-workers from Brazil called him often. Brazilians were shocked and grieving because we were continents apart.

Friends from Brazil came to visit a few days before he changed addresses to glory. Pastor Jose Assuncao, Sr. Sergio Real, Johnny Fleurte, Henrique Almeira, Kimberly and little daughter Lynli. Our Brazilian foster son, Marco Antonio Pena, arrived in time to visit with the man he called "Pai." Then he sang in Portuguese at his funeral.

Jim never lost his humor and liked to keep others entertained with his funny stories and songs. But we shared moments alone where he had tears in his eyes as he sang about heaven. Talked about his parents in heaven.

As he planned his funeral, he kept his humor. He called his elderly aunt in her 90's and told her that Tennessee Earnie Ford was going to sing at his funeral, "Come on Down, Lord Jesus".

She said, "Why, Jimmy Kemper, he already died, didn't he?"

He laughed as he held the phone. It was a bitter-sweet scene to me. Well, he did sing, by a CD!

Instead of three or four months to live as the doctors had predicted, he had two months with us after the diagnosis. He said he would like to live at least until Christmas.

Different Christmas Music

Just before Christmas 2016 his sister and brother-in-law, Judy and Jim Puckett, invited us to join them at their home for the celebration of our Lord's birth. They lived about ten miles south of us. All of their children and grandchildren were there, so were ours, Nancy and Ed Cook from Kentucky, and Rodrigo's mother and father, Mardem and Maria Ferreira and two grandsons who were visiting from Brazil.

Near the end of the evening, we gathered in the living room as Jim was seated in a chair and he sang acapella "Come on Down, Lord Jesus." Several were recording both audio and video on their phones, and there didn't seem to be any dry eyes in the house. It seemed to be his way of saying goodbye to everyone.

One More Birthday, Please

After Christmas, it was about two weeks until Jim's birthday and he made the comments that he hoped he could make it until his birthday. Well, he did.

We invited family for Jim's 79th birthday at the Ferreira's house. I wrote out a "This is Your Life, James Kemper Combs" as part of the entertainment. Funny, serious. I don't know how Jim felt hearing his life pass by, but he got serious and listened quietly. As usual, the family broke out in praise music before the night was over and their good-byes had never meant so much before.

Next, he wanted to see the new president sworn in. He was able to do that, too. In a few days he was gone.

The Last Laugh

Jim had invited Pastor Ryan Giles and Pastor Lewis Cox to participate in our celebration of his life.

Two of our children, Cindy and Kemper, shared stories of their father. Marco Antonio gave his testimony that as a street child he was taken in by our family. He sang "Milagre Sou", (I Am A Miracle).

Speakers from out-of-state that were not in Jim's plans were: Clint Morgan from International Missions; Curt Holland from IM who was "adopted" by our family while he and his family worked in Brazil; Rabbi Osvaldo Garagorry from Colorado who was our seminary student in Brazil.

A musical highlight that he didn't plan was the moment a Brazilian choir of our spiritual children from the three churches in Araras was projected bigger than life on the huge screen above the RU stage They were led by Pastor Jose Assuncao. It was a surprise for me, and I came unglued at their outpouring of love.

But Jim planned a little humor for the 500 people present. He asked me to put a tiny message in an empty walnut shell and place it in his casket. He arranged with Pastor Lewis to take out the walnut and read the message at the funeral. Pastor did that and read to us:

'"The shell is empty,

But the nut is already gone!"

Everyone laughed at Jim's last joke, and he would have been pleased.

Some commented they had never seen a funeral like his. Jim planned most of it, but his children said if he had been there, he would have complained that it was too long!

Empty Chair – New Normal

Like many other ministry widows, I started on a chapter of my 'new normal'. Fortunately, I was still healthy enough to continue many of my activities, but now I would continue without him.

The poem The BEND IN THE ROAD, by Helen Steiner Rice was sent to me, and I found it has good advice.

Sometimes we come to life's crossroads
And we view what we think is the end,
But God has a much wider vision
And He knows that it's only a bend.

The road will go on and get smoother
And after we've stopped for a rest,
The path that lies hidden beyond us
Is often the path that is best.

So, rest and relax and grow stronger,
Let go and let God share your load
And have faith in a brighter tomorrow –
You've just come to a bend in the road."

After my Bend in the Road, God seemed to add more speaking opportunities for me (instead of Jim?). I spoke at district meetings of WAC and the pastors present invited me to speak on that "same topic" at their churches. Mother's Day, Father's Day, Pastor Appreciation Sunday, Missions, Youth and Children ministries, and home groups. I loved it!!

Empty Budget

If it were not for the miracles that God did in my budget, I would not want to talk about this subject.

Four months after his passing, I was gifted with tickets to go to Brazil for three months. The Brazilian families was grieving and needed news from me.

In September when I returned, Wood Creation had downsized. So instead of working, I returned to my activities with Joy Community Choir and OASIS.

I had never really thought about how death affects your financial budget – the income drops to one half! But your insurances and taxes remain the same, and so do house payments and utility bills. You can downsize on some nonessential items, but on paper it does not balance out. How do you adjust?

Prayer. Ever since we returned to the USA I was determined to live in peace. And I did. My children volunteered to help for a while as much as they could.

In October I received a phone call from a Ms. Olga from Dallas, Texas. She offered me a job for six months for $17 an hour teaching in Moore. I accepted. My students were from Russia, France, and Ecuador. God brought a little mission field right to me.

Five months after my last job, I received another phone call. It was from Dr. Mark Brashier. Randall University was offering me a job as receptionist. I accepted. Once again God had a surprise on His list for me. The student leaders at R.U. asked me to help them host the many international students enrolled that year. Students from England, Wales, Australia, Africa, China, Mexico, and Brazil.

It reminded me that 'God so loved the world that He gave His only begotten Son…" and for that reason we were all together in Jesus' name at a Christian University.

In order to fulfill the Great Commission, the disciples received, each generation and each nation must help carry the Gospel to the ends of the Earth.

No people ever received the gospel except at the hand of an alien. W.B. Knight wrote,

"It was a Jew who brought the gospel to Rome;

A Roman who took it to France;

A Frenchman who took it to Scandinavia;

A Scandinavian who took it to Scotland;

A Scotsman who evangelized Ireland;

And an Irishman in turn made the missionary conquest of Scotland."

Because of COVID in 2020 there were many cases in the building at R.U. where I worked.

One day Pastor Mason phoned at my desk,

"Ms. Shirley, did you know you are the oldest person on this campus?"

I smiled to myself, "I had figured that out."

"There are four people in your building with COVID and we think you would be safer at your home." Many have found themselves in that situation, too.

Since then, I have not worked but I can testify that God is faithful. I volunteer at RU each week and keep busy with many wonderful things with family and ministry.

My Winter Season Passion

One of my passions during my Winter Season is to encourage prayer by sharing great answers to prayers. Including the small domestic needs and the more serious ones of freedom from evil spirits.

Many Americans don't seem to know the authority and power in the name Jesus Christ. They have not heard demons speak through the voice box of their victims and beg to not mention the name and blood of Jesus. How they scream when they have to leave the bodies of their victims by the mighty power of Jesus. Those sounds and scenes are in my memories and I have shared them in my books. Not to show the hideous and evil workings of our enemy Satan. But to show the glorious Victory for those who chose to believe in Jesus Christ, the Messiah, the Son of God.

I enjoy watching the athletic students at Randall University as they go in and out of the classroom, to chapel meetings, as they go in and out of gymnasiums, and on and off the courts and playing fields.

Their coaches make sure they stay in good physical shape with daily training. They have the physical power they need.

But it is interesting to see the arrival of the referees. They are physically fit, but they don't need to have the same physical power as the players because they have the authoritative power of the whistle and of the yellow and red flags.

Dear reader, we don't need to have the strength enough to combat the Father of Lies, because we have the authority of the Mighty Father God to call the shots.

This is better than a whistle and yellow and red flags. We can call upon the name and blood of Jesus Christ, the Son of God! I have seen and heard it firsthand. Glory, it never fails!!

My Winter Books of Miracles

Since I have left Brazil, I have continued to record and publish God's miracles to bold prayers.

In 2011 I wrote the book "Wounded Lambs Need the Fold" to reveal God at work in miraculous ways to prove His love for street children. His little lambs. I dedicated it to my parents and in-laws.

In 2013 I wrote "Who's Clapping at Our Gate?' emphasizing international hospitality and Evangelism. I dedicated it to my grandchildren.

In 2020 I wrote "This, That, and Other Miracles" which is made up of inspirational short stories of answered prayers. Stories so amazing that they are almost unbelievable. But our God is a God of miracles. It is dedicated to all the foreign missionaries who have worked in Brazil for International Missions of Free Will Baptists.

At the request of my publisher, I am writing this book during my Winter Season covering my birth to widowhood. A story of a common little nine-year-old girl from Oklahoma who surrendered her heart to Jesus Christ to be used by a powerful God who did amazing things and took her on adventures on two continents, 38 addresses. in cities, and jungles. Among the impoverished, and the wealthy. The road continues.

So far it has been an amazing journey including many addresses. 38 addresses? I had fifteen addresses while with my parents, but I was secure and grounded in a family. Many foster children have many more before they find a forever home. So don't feel sorry for me. Which city would I give up? Crowder, Berryhill, Sapulpa, Tulsa, Claremore, Owasso in my Spring season? Nashville, Kansas, Shawnee Mission, Franklin, Miamisburg, Noble, Skiatook, Sophia, Owasso, and Tulsa in my United States Summer Season? Campinas, Araras, Tubarao, or Ribeirao Preto in Brazil Summer Season? In my Autumn Season in Moore, Oklahoma with yearly trips to Brazil? So far in my Winter Season I am still in Moore, Oklahoma.

For how long? Who's counting? Life is good.

Many addresses, yes. But I already know my last one, praise God! And I know many people who will be at the same celestial address because we changed addresses may times here on this planet.

My parents sang together a song my mother called her 'testimony'.

"As we travel through this land
Many times, can't understand
Why we must keep traveling here below.
But we have this work to do
And we mean to see it through
'Til Jesus says it's time to go.
I would like to settle down
Here in this old world below,
And have a place to call my own.
But there are many lost in sin,
Someone needs to bring them in
And so I must keep traveling on.
But when the day is through
There's a home beyond the blue,
Rest and peace for all the faithful few.
I shall settle down up there
In that home so bright and fair,
That will be my bright eternal HOME!

The road goes on and on for other travelers, too, who are facing their home destination. Some will never enter their Winter Season of Life, but they will be home. What's beyond the bend? Whatever it is, God is leading. My road is leading me toward my heavenly home. I pray to see you there, too.

Father, Am I almost home?

Photos of MY Winter Season -USA

In Loving Memory

Missionary Pastor James Kemper Combs

January 13, 1938 – February 7, 2017

Brazilians bought the Headstone

Missionary James Combs

Jan. 13, 1938-Feb. 7, 2017

Friends at the Cemetery in Moore

Carolyn   Shirley   Dolores

Last of the Six Roberts Children

Shirley's Family in Moore, Oklahoma

Combs Family Reunion – West Virginia

Great Group–My children and grandchildren were there with me

RANDALL UNIVERSITY – Internationals Students

God broght the "world' to our Oklahoma door steps.

Randall University – Moore, **Ok**

International Students

Russia – France   -Russia -Columbia

il

Dayanne Correa– Puerto Rico   Renan de Lara-Brazil

Nadia Castillo, Mexico

Bruno da Silva – Brazil

The Boys from Brazil

Students also from Australia, Argentina, Germany, Tanzania, Turkey, China, Italy, South Africa, and United Kingdom

Hispanic Women's Meeting Oklahoma City

Winter Season – Brazil

Translation: "This Vehicle is an offering of love in memory of Missionary

James Kemper Combs.
A memorial on the altar of Jesus Christ."

Family Lar Nova Vida
Yearly meeting of Ex-residents and Care givers

When my time comes, I am ready to meet my Savior!

Are we almost home?

Poems and Reflections

 LIFE IS LIKE A BOOK

Life is like a book.
Each day is a new page.
Each hour is a comma.

But the pencil can't write the future and
The eraser can't blot out the past.
So, we are thankful to wake up each morning
To see there is a new page to fill.

Let us fill each page with love, joy, peace, kindness, forgiveness.
And erase any fear, bitterness, doubt, and apathy from our list.
Take good advantage of each day, because each moment is unique.
The past doesn't return and the future can't arrive.
Let us not waste our time with quarrels and bitterness.
Seek happiness and simply BE HAPPY, no matter the circumstance.

Don't be surprised to find one day your page starts a new chapter.
If God chooses a surprise title for that chapter, don't fret.
He has a perfect plan for the rest of our book.
Commit the sentences, and commas to show God's love to others.
To show there is an important life in heaven after our books are closed.

Because all of a sudden God takes the pencil and writes, "THE END."
Then We are Home!
We will find ourselves in a different dimension of time in heaven.
The pencil, the commas, the pages are left behind for posterity.
I know that one book will be opened there and our name will be searched.

I am glad I know my name is already in that Book of Life

Because I read in the greatest Book, the Bible,
That "God so loved the world that He gave His only begotten Son"
That whosever believes In Him.... will have everlasting life."
And I believed.
God continues to write on our pages. So don't take away His pen!!
Just trust the Author.

-Shirley Alberta Combs
Moore, Oklahoma, 2020

....

Note: Years ago, I read phrases in Portuguese that "*A Vida e' como um livro*" or "Life is like a book" and it caused me to meditate about it over time. Sometimes I even want to add more verses to my meditations as God writes more chapters, but I will just leave the pen in the hands of the Author.

Note: Before leaving for Brazil the first time in 1964, Jim and I traveled across the US sharing with folks the vision of God for the world and how we and they fit into that plan. Since Jim is from the state of West Virginia, we visited many friends and churches there.

One day we received a letter and this poem from Mrs. Thelma I. Pack from Ansted, West Virginia. She wrote that she penned this poem in 1964 and dedicated it to us. It was emotional to us to see our names in the poem. That was almost 60 years ago at this writing and it has blessed us as we left and returned many times.

A DEDICATED LIFE

(For Shirley and Jim)
How many are willing in this life to go
Across the deep waters, God's love to show,
To deny oneself and carry the rugged cross
To every nation that here might still be lost?

Many are great – but still some are small,
But yet they have heard and answered the call
To go from home and kindred so dear
For souls in foreign countries, they gospel might hear.

There is a man and his name is called **JIM**
Who is willing to give all-God's favor to win,
SHIRLEY, his wife, who stands by his side
To go to foreign mission with God as their guide.

Oh, it won't be easy, there is no doubt
And Satan will try hard to make them back out.
But lost are at stake and who will dare go
To tell them of Jesus and His love to them show?

There have been some who have paid with their life
To tell them of Jesus the crucified Christ
For Jesus Himself his own life did give
That all who believe forever can live.

I dedicate this to Shirley and Jim

Who have dedicated all, lost souls to win.
Someday in Heaven at the end of the way
A payday is coming as they hear Jesus say...

Come enter in! A crown you have won.
Well done, He will say, for the work you have done.
It will be worth all the time you both did give.
For the joys of heaven and with Jesus to live.

Note: On Friday the 13th. As I was coming out from under anesthesia after an outpatient surgery, this story came to my mind. Like a dream I could see how people were dressed, the boss behind the counter, the customers. A young mother and children are entering the door. When the thought came "write it down", I thought, I record real stores and not fiction. The thought came again, "Write it in poetry form." I reached for a notebook and pencil from my night stand. I tried to focus on what was going through my head. I still felt drowsy, but I recognized the Voice in my head and have never been disappointed for obeying it before. The story started unfolding quickly in rhyming words and I started writing. This is the first time I have shared it. Enjoy the message.

(A young mother and children stop at a popular, and modern truck stop and quietly enter the business.)

The Boss's Good Day

A neatly dressed lady walked in that day,
Told her little children to close-by stay.
And the boss at the counter heard the mother say:
"Sir, I'm here to make a humble request.
It's really not the thing that I do best."
She talked quietly, but the customers heard,
And discreetly stopped to hear her words.
"I can clean your restrooms
And your floors with a broom
In exchange for my kids a little food."
The boss looked around at customers there,
And ran his hand through his thinning hair.
"Lady, have the kids sit in the chairs.
I'm sure we have food that we can share."
Reach out! Embrace! Together we can share.
Reach out! Embrace! Show a stranger that we care.
The woman said:
"Thanks, sir. I have food at home.
Money there, debit cards, and cell phone.
But we left there quickly, with just some gas,
To leave our pain and danger in the past.
My husband died in the distant war.
So, we live with kin we didn't know before."
The mother and kids sat and bowed heads in prayer.
The customers couldn't help but kindly stare.
A trucker at the counter waiting to pay,
Said, "Here's for the lady to help in some way."
A couple went to the family in chairs.
"Our church has a prophet's room. You can stay there."
Reach out! Embrace! Together we can share.

Reach out! Embrace! Show a stranger that we care .
The woman said:
"My godly parents don't live very far.
Tomorrow, I can reach them soon by car.
As soon as I clean for this kind man,
Then I'm free to safely follow the plan."
The boss at the counter looked at the scene,
"Ah, I'm sure the rooms and floors are clean."
She smiled and nodded, called her kids from the chairs
And the customers felt a special moment they shared.
Strangers hugged, and went on their way.
A mother and children in their car just prayed.
And the boss?
Profits? Sales? Nothing compares in any way
To the goodwill the boss could see that day!
Chorus: **Reach out! Embrace! Bring mercy from above.**
Reach out! Embrace! The world needs unselfish love.
-Shirley Combs

4. Father, Are We Almost Home?

(A late-night chat with the Father)

I love our times of talk, Father, even when my thoughts are scattered.

Each candle on my cake lights up a new season of my life.

The challenges of life were hidden from me, but not to my Lord Jesus.

Sometimes I faced them with silence, sometimes crying on my knees.

Many days were crowned with joy, but at times only He saw my tears, Father.

You sent me to give to others your best, and for my good, you took things from me.

You gave me beautiful memories that faded the scars on my soul.

We both smiled when faith accepted your best,

And were relieved when forgiveness removed their doubts.

For years I have put my impossibilities on your list and your miracles have answered.

I have put more things on your list, but will I see them answered before we arrive home?

Are we almost home, Father?

I love my family here on earth united, but will my family Circle up there be unbroken?

My heart aches while I am waiting and praying, but I want to speak truth, live truth enough.

For your power is enough to stand against the enemy who wants to deceive and steal family away.

May the enemy lose his grip and the young and old will lose their doubts and fears.

I pray that each family member will know the joy that trusting you can bring.

While *we wait* upon more candles, you *renew* our strength!

We have mounted *upon wings* of earthly planes with good news of your salvation miracles.

We have run down the cobblestone streets and *we're not weary*.

We found adventure on the dusty roads, and *didn't faint*.

You are the sustainer of creation and

You haven't forgotten the sparrow,

and You take good care of me.

My goal is to reach there with You one day,

and hear "Welcome home, my child",

With your love my journey has been blessed.

You didn't promise a nonstop flight on my way.

But each earthly address brought me closer to home.

Am I almost there?

Are we almost home, Father?

-Shirley Combs, 6-27-22

Made in the USA
Middletown, DE
06 June 2023

31829974R00186